Long Weekends

RICK STEIN'S
Long Weekends

BBC
BOOKS

This book is dedicated to Ed, Jack and Charlie and Sas, Zach and Olive

10 9 8 7 6 5 4 3 2 1

BBC Books, an imprint of Ebury Publishing
20 Vauxhall Bridge Road
London SW1V 2SA

BBC Books is part of the Penguin Random House
group of companies whose addresses can be found
at global.penguinrandomhouse.com

 Penguin
Random House
UK

This book is published to accompany the television
series entitled *Rick Stein's Long Weekends* first
broadcast on BBC Two in 2016. *Rick Stein's Long
Weekends* is a Denhams production.

Producer and director: David Pritchard
Associate producer: Arezoo Farahzad
Executive producer for the BBC: Lindsey Bradbury

First published by BBC Books in 2016

www.eburypublishing.co.uk

A CIP catalogue record for this book is available
from the British Library

ISBN 9781785940927

Printed and bound by
Firmengruppe APPL, aprinta druck, Wemding, Germany

Penguin Random House is committed to a
sustainable future for our business, our readers
and our planet. This book is made from Forest
Stewardship Council® certified paper.

 MIX
Paper from
responsible sources
FSC® C018179
FSC
www.fsc.org

Commissioning editor: Lizzy Gray
Project editor: Mari Roberts
Editor: Charlotte Macdonald
Design and art direction: Smith & Gilmour
Photographer: James Murphy
Food stylist: Aya Nishimura
Assistant food stylists: Tamara Vos,
Charlotte O'Connell and Nicola Roberts
Prop stylist: Penny Markham

INTRODUCTION

'Hey, Rick, where're you going this weekend?'

There's nothing quite so exciting as the prospect of flying off somewhere for the weekend. You can forget the bills, the schools, the illness of friends, and just go. A quick flight to Bordeaux, maybe, with the thought of some aged ribs of beef cooked over vine prunings, and all those lovely Bordelais wines in elegant, straight-sided bottles, the tantalizing blends of Cabernet Sauvignon, Merlot and Cabernet Franc for the reds and Sauvignon Blanc and Sémillon for the whites, with some sea bass and beurre blanc also in the offing.

It's extra special if you can get Friday afternoon off. From London, Cardiff, Belfast or Edinburgh, you could get on a plane and that night be sitting in a bar in Cadiz, such as Casa Manteca, ordering a Cruzcampo beer and a serving of chicharrones (page 148), cold belly pork cooked with garlic and cumin seeds and sprinkled with lemon juice and coarse salt, which arrive in long thin slices on a sheet of greaseproof paper. Equally you might find yourself in the back streets of Palermo at the Vucciria market, where a fisherman in wellington boots is boiling octopus, all purple in a black pot, and he pulls one out with tongs, slices a few thick white tentacles on to a paper plate and adds a couple of lemon wedges, and you wander over to a table in a bar to eat them, salty and hot and smelling of seawater. The fisherman goes back to a white plastic seat to watch his boiling pot and you survey the confusion that is Sicily's capital. To your right is a dirty, empty building, its windows filled in with concrete blocks, but they still have ornate balconies and carved window surrounds. Across from you is a bar not yet open with jagged graffiti scrawled all over it. An old table football game in faded red and cream stands outside on the square, and big green rectangular rubbish bins line up in ranks.

You'll find no such thing on a long weekend in Iceland. Instead, you will get cod so fresh it's almost tough to the bite, or langoustine tails in a soup made with bisque from the shells (page 57), flavoured with such a tiny pinch of curry powder that it's just a whisper at the back of your taste buds. You could take off to Vienna and settle down for a lunch of *Tafelspitz* (page 254), the most comforting combination of thickly sliced boiled beef with horseradish and a pile of carrots, swede and leeks, all cooked with the beef and served with buttery rösti potatoes and a plate of marrow bones, roasted and dark from the oven, which you scoop out and spread on rye bread.

The intention of this book is twofold. First, to persuade you to go to Bordeaux, Berlin, Reykjavik, Vienna, Bologna, Copenhagen, Cadiz, Lisbon,

Thessaloniki and Palermo, because I've been to these cities and I can tell you that you will find much to enjoy there. It's not just about going away for a long weekend, however. It's also a book about the pleasures of cooking at the weekend at home. When I was a boy in the 1950s, there was a book in our holiday home on Trevose Head in Cornwall called *The Week-End Book*. It first came out in the 1930s. The book had sections on early-morning bird calls, indoor and outdoor games, maps of the summer stars, poetry, songs with the musical score for piano accompaniment, dance steps with little black and white footprints, and weekend recipes, which were introduced with the advice: 'Week-end cookery should be either very quick, a good meal produced in half an hour, or very slow, to put on before you go to tennis or to lazing.' It's a memory for me of happy times in our house looking over the bay to Mother Ivey's beach, playing deck quoits on the grass outside the sitting room waiting for lobster, mayonnaise and new potatoes for supper.

I think weekends are a time for memories. So this is my weekend book. I brought back about ten recipes from each of the cities and have worked them into a series of chapters based on how I like to cook at the weekend. What I do on Friday night after a long week is quick and easy, what I like to do on Saturday breakfast is quite substantial and more inclined to brunch and so on, then some serious entertaining on Saturday night, a light breakfast on Sunday morning, a classic Sunday lunch, and something conciliatory and comforting on a Sunday night to calm the mind and enjoy a last few hours of relaxation before the turbulent week ahead. Included, too, is a chapter on things to go with afternoon tea, as well as some recipes that require serious attention, the sort of things I might have found in *The Week-end Book* if it hadn't been so British-based. Things like making sauerkraut and sourdough bread, or an extraordinary vegan uncooked lasagne from a cook called Solla Eiríksdóttir in Iceland, which sounds dreadful but tastes wonderful. Recipes you might well do at the weekend when you've got more time.

However, since this book is also about the places I've been, here follows a flavour of my ten cities: not so much the big virtues of each, but more an attempt to colour in a little detail.

BORDEAUX was the natural choice as the first city for my long weekends. We'd filmed there about ten years earlier as part of my series *French Odyssey*, and I know it well from quite a few visits to Château Bauduc, owned by Gavin and Angela Quinney, who make one of our biggest-selling house wines. It's one of the perks of the restaurant business that one often feels the necessity to visit some attractive part of France, Spain or Italy to check on the latest vintage and try one or two bottles, and visit some well-loved restaurant such as La Tupina in Bordeaux at the same time. It is a perfect city for a short visit. It's almost as if it's been spruced up for that precise purpose. It used to be called *La Belle Endormie*, 'Sleeping Beauty', referring to the magnificence of the buildings hidden in dirt and grime from years of pollution. The largely eighteenth-century centre with not a high-rise building in sight stands on the left (south) bank of the Garonne river. Viewed from across the water it's like a stage set, an affirmation of everything you like about France. You just know you're going to find things to eat and drink that will confirm this. I remember having breakfast at a café on the river near the Pont de Pierre, Napoleon's famous bridge, whose seventeen arches are supposed to correspond to the seventeen letters in 'Napoleon Bonaparte', and thinking that this was entirely as it should be: a cup of dark, highly roasted *café au lait* and a *tartine beurrée*, and lengthways slices of baguette and Échiré butter with French marmalade, which always tastes sweeter and less bitter than ours.

With Bordeaux, you have not just the city to wander around, but also some of the world's most famous wine-growing villages and areas around it. Saint-Émilion, Saint-Julien, Saint-Estèphe, Pauillac and Graves et Sauternes – the names flood me with memories of great food and wine. You've got to go and have lunch in Margaux or Lalande-de-Pomerol. The wine lists are usually a sweet confusion of names famous and unknown, and you almost always end up asking for help. I like to keep the food simple to go with it. Maybe an *entrecôte bordelaise* or a bowl of mussels with Bayonne ham or Dover sole cooked *à la meunière*. There will be time, too, to make it to the coast, maybe Cap Ferrat for a plate of tiny bouchot mussels (rope-grown), or to Arcachon, where a number of fish restaurants line the beach, all overlooking a sculpture of a whale diving into the deep, its vast tail in the air, which they paint a different colour every season. It was red when I went.

We arrived in **BERLIN** in cold rain and darkness. No wonder David, the director, and I began to call it very *noir*: dark places and a dark history, with the Jewish monument prominent in the centre. Actually you can tell from the trees everywhere and from the Tiergarten, the large park right in the centre that was once a hunting ground, that it would be a very different place in the summer. But part of the outcome of the pressure for us to get filming quickly was that we had to go to some cities, Vienna, Reykjavik and Bologna as well as Berlin, in the darker, wetter, colder months, which I think added greatly to the overall effect of our trips. Simply put, you don't want to restrict your weekend trips to the summer. Berlin is a city bursting with energy, a young city, and in spite of its history it doesn't feel like a capital atrophied by its past. It's a place of endless possibilities, partly I think because it's cheap to live there: rents are low and young people can open bars, clubs and restaurants, sometimes in the most improbable places, like an old brewery, or a couple of floors in a building in the service area behind a large hotel, or a place in a rough part of town with no visible sign outside that a very cutting-edge restaurant is within. On one occasion, we filmed a function in an old crematorium. It's a fabulous place for a weekend.

I can understand why many people find German food heavy and unattractive but I think it's similar to our own in the sense that it's nourishing food for cold climates, with plenty of meat, poultry and carbohydrates and, like our own, is worth taking seriously. If, like me on one occasion, you find yourself consumed by hunger and thirst, you might find cheer in the arrival of a vast plate of *Eisbein*, pork knuckle with sauerkraut and split yellow peas, and a large glass of Berliner Pilsner at a restaurant like Zur Letzten Instanz, the oldest in Berlin. The name, 'At the Highest Court', refers to a legal dispute between two farmers, who eventually settled not in court but over a beer in the pub. Much as I love a good pork knuckle boiled or grilled, it is quite a challenge to eat, which is why I've changed my recipe on page 252 to use a smaller piece of cured belly pork.

The idea of making classic German food a little less calorific crops up quite often in Berlin itself. In one restaurant, La Soupe Populaire, I opted for a traditional favourite: Königsberger Klopse (page 204). Delightful light, fluffy meatballs in a sauce made with chicken stock, cream and *Beerenauslese* Riesling arrived, with the smoothest mashed potato, which I had watched being passed through the finest of sieves. It was accompanied by a beetroot salad flavoured delicately with Tabasco sauce (page 204). Like Copenhagen, though, you must seek out those restaurants where the new breed of young chefs are cooking food using only ingredients grown or reared locally. Sometimes it can be a bit wacky – roasted dandelion buds with sunflower-seed gravy, for example – but they're on to something, as Billy Wagner, proprietor of the unforgettably named Nobelhart & Schmutzig explained: 'I'm thirty-five. My parents loved to cook with anything Mediterranean: tomatoes, peppers, lemons, olive oil, so to me that's what I grew up with. What excites me is using German ingredients: beetroot, cabbage, horseradish, lard and butter.'

The prospect of going to **REYKJAVIK** got me into a panic. There would be nothing good to eat and no recipes for my book. Tales of stinky skate, rotten shark, bull's testicles and whale blubber worried me further. I read about the tough times the Icelanders had had in the past trying to survive in a country once described as 'somewhat north of life'. At one time the population ate seaweed and moss to supplement their meagre diet. At least, I reasoned, the fish would be good, and I might find something else half decent to eat. In fact, it turned out there was plenty of perfectly good food, and finding truly memorable dishes didn't matter as much as I'd thought because the country is so magnificent, the people are so friendly and it's so different from anywhere else I've ever been.

Flying over Iceland in winter and being lucky enough to get fine weather was just the start of it. It looks such a remote, white wilderness, with jagged black mountains, clearly volcanic by their very sharp lines, and water everywhere, dark lakes in shadow and zigzags of rivers and streams. As the plane turned for the final approach into Reykjavik, the sun shone on miles of blue sea inlets and islands. Trundling my case out of the airport, it was all slippery black ice and the growing realization that my coat was too thin for the sub-zero temperature and the cutting wind. The city is tiny, about 200,000 inhabitants, but it's partly the small size that makes you feel so welcome. I could walk everywhere, and the wood and corrugated-iron houses gaily painted in dark blues, yellows, reds and greens added to the human scale of the place. Sitting in the warm bar of my hotel right on the harbour, wearing my newly purchased blue and white sheep's wool sweater smelling of lanolin, I watched a local barman with New York-style aplomb making a cocktail featuring a large quantity of the local caraway aquavit, Brennivín. This display was enhanced by the presence through the window not twenty metres away of a bright red trawler propped up on stilts on the shore, having winter repairs. Driving out the next day to a farm seventy miles west, we stopped off by a lake, half of which was frozen, the other half warm with thermal steam coming up through the sand, where a man called Rasmussen had buried a pot of sweet rye dough twenty-four hours earlier and was digging it up to slice, butter and hand over to me, along with a plate of thinly sliced smoked sea trout from the same lake.

The food scene in Reykjavik is exciting. Stick to the fish anywhere and all will be fine, but there are also some young chefs who echo what is happening in Denmark. Both countries have similar cuisines, since Iceland was part of Denmark from 1814 till 1918. The cuisine was not always inspiring but it has given them a clean slate to invent something new.

I had to go back to **VIENNA**. I'd been there just before Christmas about five years ago with Sas, my wife. We stayed near the Naschmarkt, the central market which, in addition to having lots of very good butchers, fishmongers, cheese and fruit and vegetable stores, also has a famous sauerkraut shop, featuring immense open-topped barrels of the pungent, sour, caraway-smelling cabbage. You can buy it from reasonably fresh to well aged. For me, sauerkraut is like aged wine, not in taste, of course, but in the way the flavours become more fascinating the older it gets. It's also a great place to eat outdoors, and you only have to cross the street to walk past the Secession Building with its clean white lines and the giant ball of gold-leaf work on its roof. It's my favourite building in the city, some say far more impressive than the gallery it houses, though not me because I love Klimt's paintings, and within is a frieze he painted to celebrate Beethoven's Ninth Symphony. Then to go on to the opera to see *Daphne* by Richard Strauss – I can think of no better, more atmospheric accompaniment to a long weekend in Vienna. Like Mahler, Strauss' pastoral romanticism is reflected to me in the sense of order and classical proportion in the buildings in the city. You can sit in faded cafés over a single Melange coffee and read the paper for an hour or so while others around you are writing or having what seem to be philosophical discussions and everyone is dressed conservatively.

There's very little cutting-edge cuisine in Vienna but they've got plenty to be proud of in their culinary traditions. To be able to go to the Imperial Hotel and watch the perfect Wiener Schnitzel (page 198) being made, then sit down with Martina Hohenlohe, editor-in-chief of the Austrian Gault et Millau, and discuss the essential points of the dish while enjoying a glass of Grüner Veltliner, or to watch the almost film-set theatricality at the Demel patisserie of a line of Sachertorte (page 114) being flooded with shining dark chocolate – all this is fascinating. When we filmed in Vienna I tried a piece about Grahame Greene's *The Third Man* but it didn't really come off. It's not a work of his I like, being in essence a film script, and a description of then postwar Vienna, all seedy and poor, which is not how I see the city. No, what counts for me is the grand Baroque architecture, the palaces, some of which look as though they've been built out of sugar, and the elegant gardens, such as at the Belvedere.

In **BOLOGNA**, perhaps the most extraordinary feature is the collection of twelfth-century towers, built, it is said, by feuding families, but whether to gain the advantage for shooting at each other or simply as a statement of family wealth, no one is sure. Either way, they are a sombre and enigmatic presence. At one time there were getting on for a hundred; now there are about twenty. The remaining ones include the two most famous, the Asinelli, and next to it, much lower and almost leaning against it, the Garisenda, which together form the strange emblem of this beautiful city.

Walking into the city centre is like walking into a Renaissance world. I almost expected to see a couple of bearded men walk across the Piazza Maggiore wearing felt hats, billowy shirts, doublets, breeches, hose and leather boots, with rapiers at their waists. The city has forty kilometres of porticos, so that the streets are bordered by elegant arcades, often with ornately carved arches and ochre-red ceilings and walls. It rained most of the time I was there but I only got briefly wet when crossing the street from one civilized covered walkway to the next. The porticos were mostly built in the late Middle Ages under pressure for space within the confines of a walled city. Owners were able to commandeer space on the pavements to erect columns to support rooms above. The effect is to make all the streets narrow, adding to the medieval feeling.

It is one of the oldest cities in Italy, housing Europe's first university. Walking through you feel unjustifiably intellectual, as if the ancient seat of learning is rubbing off on you, and the cooking is entirely in keeping. Being the capital of Emilia-Romagna, which has in the Po basin some of the best farming land in Europe, the cooking is rich and satisfying. The local red wines are not full-bodied and complex but designed to counterbalance the richness of all that Parmesan cheese, Parma ham, culatello and the calorific meat sauces for pasta. I'm thinking particularly of Sangiovese and Lambrusco wines, which don't suit ageing, and are full of dark fruit with acidity and tannin and, in the case of the latter, often a sparkle. Thank goodness those sweet Lambruscos of the 1970s, which we all drank, not especially gratefully, are a memory.

Bologna for me was a time of lots of rain, so all the more reason to sit in restaurants and bars eating many variations of the soft, deep yellow, homemade egg pasta Bologna is so famous for – tagliatelle, ravioli, tortelloni, tortellini to name but a few – and to be continually reminded of the closeness of Parma ham, culatello, Parmesan. A trip out of the tight circular world of the old town to a Parmesan maker in the snowy hills nearby was welcome not just for a breath of ice air but also for being the first to taste the centre of a three-year-old cheese, just as it was split open. It abounded with the crunchy crystals typical of the best, but also had a salty fragrance both fresh and old at the same time. The sort of taste that fills you with a sense of arriving not just at the centre of the cheese but at the still point of the turning world of cheese.

The presence of both prosciutto and Parmesan in so much Bolognese food is impossible to resist, which is why I would like to direct you to Cotoletta alla Bolognese on page 276. And, yes, I'll have a Sangiovese with it.

COPENHAGEN, wonderful Copenhagen, the salty old queen of the sea I'd like to call her – because there is a saltiness about this city by the Baltic, and a femininity too. There's a sense of cooperation about the place. It's got the narrowest gap between rich and poor in the world and the least corruption and it's one of the happiest cities anywhere.

It's not big on testosterone, it's big on practicality. It's almost flat, so, sensibly, the most popular form of transport is the bicycle, and they're not 'my bike is bigger and better than yours' bikes. There's almost a standard Copenhagen cycle: comfortable seat and an extra bracing-bar running diagonally from front to the back so it works for both men and women, few gears, straight handlebars and practical brakes, too, the main one you engage by back-pedalling. You wear your ordinary clothes to ride it, not Lycra with padded bottoms. It's just a bike. Saltiness abounds in the food, too, most notably in the fish. Their ways with curing herring are many. In one of the central markets I counted no less than twelve different types of salted and cured herring, not to mention salmon, trout, halibut and eel, all salted, or salted and smoked.

I first went to Copenhagen twelve years ago and was charmed by the human scale of the city. No high buildings, and harbours and canals with houseboats on either side, and lining the canals trees and pretty, painted houses. I didn't rave about the food then, except for the *smørrebrød* (page 93), the open ryebread sandwiches, usually with herring or smoked salmon, prawns or rare beef, with dill and horseradish sour cream, beetroot and often mayonnaise or remoulade. This time the new Nordic cooking revolution had happened. Restaurants like Noma, Geranium and Kadeau were adorned with Michelin stars and eschewed any ingredients that weren't local. I went to quite a few of them, and found the dishes ranged from exciting and innovative to a slight sensation of being in Hans Christian Andersen's story 'The Emperor's New Clothes'.

Returning to safe ground on the last day of my visit I went to a restaurant called Gammel Mønt and watched Claus Christensen poach a whole turbot in a copper turbot kettle and accompany it with a simple sauce of butter and lemon and a whole pile of pointed cabbage cooked in more butter with lemon juice and nutmeg (page 190), and I have to say I was massively enthusiastic, especially as we drank a magnum of chilled Savennières with it. Maybe it was like finally finding my shirt and trousers.

'…lying curved on the bay like a scimitar and sparkling with African light'

Laurie Lee captured the feeling of **CADIZ** for me as I drove in one evening when the sun was setting. Even today, the city is still a low line along the bay. From the moment you drive towards it you feel you're somewhere between Europe and Africa, particularly when the Levant wind blows in from Morocco, warm and humid. There is a scent of something unfamiliar in the air. As you get closer to the old city, the strangeness is accentuated. Why is it so different to anywhere else? It's as marvellous in its way as Venice. Then you get it: it's surrounded by the sea. It's on a strip of land out in the bay, not the bay itself. Unlike most old cities it can't be surrounded by out-of-town shopping centres, crane yards, car showrooms and modern blocks of flats because it's right on the Atlantic Ocean. You see it much as it would have looked in the fifteenth or sixteenth century.

You walk through narrow streets filled with a sherry bodega here, a mini supermarket there, with a tumble of plastic buckets, oranges, tomatoes and lemons outside, and a dark bar with two old men drinking wine, then you emerge from one labyrinth into a beautiful square awash with bougainvillea, with the buildings white and chrome yellow, and an old church or palace with small-paned casement windows above you. You just have to sit at a table and order a *café con leche* and a glass of sparkling water and think how happy you are to be back in Spain. You know there will be something red and yellow for lunch, something a bit spicy and garlicky maybe, with that nutty taste of sherry and bitter olive oil. Near La Plaza de Mina I found a tapas bar called Ultramar & Nos. On the stove in the kitchen were three dishes, one of which was a chickpea, chorizo and *pimentón* stew (page 42), whose recipe had come from the owner's mother. I washed it down with two glasses of manzanilla, and it seemed to sum up my feelings about Cadiz.

Hurry to Cadiz. Stay in a seaside holiday hotel in June, swim in the just warm enough Atlantic every day and order the fabulous seasonal Almadraba tuna in any way: sashimi, chargrilled, sautéed, stewed with red wine or served with lashings of slowly stewed onions. You will feel that this is a phantasmagorical place between the sea and the blue sky.

Cities like Lisbon and Palermo are places in which to feel fascinated by bustling, bristling human life, like Indian cities but far less extreme, places that haven't lost their soul.

Cervejaria Ramiro is not in the best part of **LISBON** town. When you join the long queue to get a table, someone from Angola or Mozambique will try to sell you a phone case or a selfie stick or a sort of flashing plastic thing. Once through the door, it's very noisy, very bright, slightly disorientating. There are shellfish tanks, a long bar with the kitchen right behind and waiters gliding the most colourful plates of seafood over the heads of diners. The beer pump seems to be permanently on. If you order beer it comes in small ice-cold glasses and as you drink three-quarters of it another appears. If you don't want more, you have to tell them, otherwise it keeps on coming. It is a *cervejaria* after all, a beer house selling seafood. I suggest you order a plate of peeled prawns fried in olive oil, butter, chilli and coriander. Maybe follow with some *carabineros*, dark red prawns from 200 metres deep in the Atlantic between Portugal and Morocco, or perhaps some giant langoustines just boiled in salty water, or a pile of murex, spiky sea snails whose shells gave us the colour purple in Roman times – for dyeing only the togas of emperors, so rare and expensive was it. The crabs and lobsters are just boiled, the sardines and dorado are grilled straight from the ocean, but the thing not to miss is the 'dessert': a little in-joke. It's a thin slice of salty veal steak brushed with oil, salt and garlic, grilled and served in a heavenly rustic bun.

Anyone who has lived in Lisbon will have memories of places like this. Little seafood bars and restaurants along narrow streets, with glimpses of the wide blue Tagus river and the sea beyond. It's a city built on hills, its structures old and slightly crumbling, with a friendly atmosphere of bustle along its streets of houses, warehouses and flats faced with faded tiles in pale blues, greens and browns. It's not driven by the price of property so there are interesting little shops and tucked-away cafés. A lesson, I think, on the downside of prosperity and success, in a city where you can live not too expensively and feel at home.

If you like a good tourist spot, I recommend the Belém tower right at the mouth of the river, a sixteenth-century fort built to guard the river. It's a memorable example of the Portuguese late Gothic architecture known as Manueline, all intricate turrets and crenellations with heraldic shields in stone, an ornateness that speaks of wealth flowing in from all those colonies, and influences from the style of 'new' places such as India, as well as a celebration of things maritime, both shells from the seas and ropes from the ships. It means a lot to the Portuguese for it was the last sight the sailors would have seen before setting out on their journeys of discovery: to the Americas, Africa, the Indies and China, leaving their loved ones behind.

The street food of **PALERMO** is not without some challenges: spleen sandwiches are popular, as are grilled intestines. It's good to be in a city where they still eat robust food. There are not many places you can go to in the UK to eat faggots or eel pie and mash these days. Maybe I'm a little odd in liking such apparently unpleasant things, but I do. It's a question of seizing the moment, making a shift, jumping in and enjoying, for example, the hardness of pasta in Palermo, with a sauce of cauliflower, olive oil, garlic and pecorino cooked so long that the florets are almost falling apart into a purée, then sprinkled with fried breadcrumbs, not Parmesan (page 30). Maybe in Palermo, too, you might try a simple bun split and sandwiched back together with a straight-out-of-the-fryer fritter of chickpea flour and fennel seeds (page 151), or radicchio stewed until it's almost black in olive oil. That's the way it is in Palermo.

But walking along those slightly seedy streets, nearly everywhere you go are signs of a glorious past, a crumbling balcony here, weeds growing out of the joins in the fluted stone columns of an elaborate portico there. There is always a sense of grandeur about the city. It feels like a capital. Even more so if you travel the nine miles or so from the centre of Palermo to Monreale and visit the fabulous Norman cathedral there, built by William the Second of Normandy. The Byzantine mosaics are breathtaking. The combination of Byzantium, Normandy and Arab there seem to be echoed in the city itself, not only in the buildings but in markets. The Ballarò market feels more like it's based somewhere in North Africa or the Middle East than Europe. It sprawls along several streets behind the Via Maqueda, a blaze of colour from all the fruit and vegetable stands, with sheets of plywood resting on crates for counters. As I wound through the narrow streets in the spring when I was there I saw green piles of young artichokes, broccoli, peas and French and broad beans; off-the-tree oranges and lemons still with leaves on them; red peppers, some still shaded with green; round aubergines and deep purple oval ones, and boxes of early marmande striped tomatoes, the ones they rasp on to bread with olive oil and garlic. Great trunks of tuna and *espada* (swordfish) and smudged silver belts of scabbard fish, and sardines a-plenty with firm bellies and scales slipping off. Counters, too, of tinned salted anchovies, the salt brown from the cure, and blocks of *mosciame*, salted and dried tuna that you grate on to pasta. The market traders are a mix of European and African. There's talk of clearing the market out and building a hygienic, covered facility. Get there before it's too late.

I asked Evdokia Tsatsouri how she would sum up why **THESSALONIKI** was such a special place. 'It's a city with a soul,' she said without hesitation. She went on to compare Greece's second largest city with the first, Athens, which she said was faster and harsher. We were being filmed walking down some steps in the Ano Poli, the old city, into a little square named after the city's most famous rebetiko artist, Vasilis Tsitsanis. Behind us was the rather gloomy former prison, held to be the birthplace of the haunting songs and deeply felt dancing that express the pain and oppression of poverty and the longing of love. Rebetiko is to the Thessalonians what fado is to the people of Lisbon. Even in the modern city there's more to be soulful about than meets the eye. Times are hard. Unemployment in the under-thirties is running at 50 per cent, but it's a city where you feel alive. There's a great sense of community. It's almost as if the hard times have brought people together in a determination to enjoy living in such a beautiful part of the world. Evdokia, rather like a Greek goddess herself, was our guide, recommending all those lesser-known tavernas, ouzerias and cafés that are the lifeblood of our *Long Weekends* series. Places like To Elliniko (The Hellenic) in Kallari Street, where we went twice to eat the shallots stuffed with minced lamb, pine nuts, cumin and cinnamon (page 139), so good were they, or a taverna on the beach at Epanomi, just beyond the airport, called The Anchor, where I swam and ate grilled tsipoura (gilt-head bream), my pale blue wooden chair gradually becoming lopsided as one leg sank into the sand, tipping me over.

Thessaloniki is a lovely city crammed full of history in the form of the ruins of Byzantine palaces and Roman arches sandwiched between modern blocks of flats in a gloriously haphazard fashion. There's music and laughter in the streets and the restaurants are full. The promenade along the waterfront is crowded with young people in the warm early evening; to walk it in the welcome breeze from the sea is a must. It's a youthful city, filled with students, about 150,000 of them, and you want to share in their excitement and the youthful optimism they feel in spite of the hard times. One way to do this is to enjoy some of the best cooking in Greece, influenced by the city's position in the fertile north, a part of the world marked by influences from the rest of Greece, the Balkans and, historically, some exotic cross-pollination from Byzantium and hundreds of years of Ottoman rule.

FRIDAY NIGHT

GREEN RICE WITH GARLIC PARSLEY, CLAMS & PRAWNS 24

MUSSEL PILAF WITH CINNAMON, CUMIN & SAFFRON 28

DANISH FISH FRIKADELLER WITH REMOULADE 29

SICILIAN PASTA WITH CAULIFLOWER, ANCHOVIES, CURRANTS & PINE NUTS 30

PRAWNS & CLAMS WITH GARLIC & CORIANDER 34

SIMPLE COD GRATIN WITH BEARNAISE SAUCE TOPPING 35

FENNEL & SAUSAGE RAGÙ WITH TAGLIATELLE 38

SPAGHETTI ALLA BOLOGNESE 39

ICELANDIC BREADED LAMB CHOPS WITH SPICED RED CABBAGE 40

CHICKPEA WITH CHORIZO TAPAS 42

CHICKEN WITH MARSALA 43

KOZANI CHICKEN WITH PRUNES, SAFRON & PAPRIKA 46

'Monday, I have Friday on my mind'
THE EASYBEATS

Each day of the week feels differently to all of us. Monday, maybe, there's a little residue of a great weekend when your efficiency can be slightly impaired. Monday night's dinner will probably be diet-conscious, with certainly no beer or wine. Tuesday is back to normal and it's great to feel fit again. Wednesday I'm going places and the healthy diet continues except that I always need to meet my oldest friends for a pint or two at the Cornish Arms that night. Thursday a little ennui creeps in at work. Everything seems interminable and there may be a dinner somewhere that night to compensate. On Friday, however, with the prospect of the weekend, things happen at work, efficiency is incredible, work really is done in the time given. Decisions always seem to get made on a Friday afternoon.

Coming from someone who's spent much of his life working in restaurant kitchens, it might seem odd to be writing about how the pace of life and indeed what one eats differs from day to day through the week. In a busy kitchen, surely, any day is the same? Actually, it's not. Each corresponds to the way other people feel about the week, especially Friday night. In the early restaurant days, I'd often get in for the evening service with the excitement of a full restaurant all weekend and change the entire menu, brimming with euphoria, much to the dismay of the rest of the kitchen. Not a good idea, and nor is it a good idea to get complicated with a Friday night's cooking at home. You could almost call these recipes thirty-minute meals after a hectic week. Just such a recipe would be the Prawns and Clams with Garlic and Coriander from Lisbon on page 34. You couldn't want for a simpler or more exciting recipe. It was Friday night when I was filmed eating that dish in Cervejaria Ramiro, a seafood and beer place, with lots of bread to soak up the garlic and chilli oil. Switch from summer to a cold and hard winter Friday evening and think of lamb chops cut from the best end, egged and breaded and fried in butter with a slow-cooked red cabbage (Icelandic Breaded Lamb Chops on page 40), from Reykjavik. The sort of thing to warm you with comfort as you come in from an icy, cutting wind on the road home.

ARROZ VERDE
GREEN RICE *WITH* GARLIC, PARSLEY, CLAMS & PRAWNS

=== SERVES FOUR TO FIVE ===

This is my take on a dish I had in Cadiz at a restaurant called La Marea (The Tide), which specializes in seafood and rice. It is one for garlic lovers, particularly as I – untypically for Spain – like to serve it with alioli as well.

60ml olive oil
60g shallots,
    finely chopped
12 cloves garlic,
    finely chopped
1 litre *Fish stock* (page 307)
100g flat-leaf parsley,
    leaves finely chopped
1½ tsp salt
400g short-grain paella
    rice, such as Calasparra
30 raw clams, preferably
    palourdes (vongole),
    scrubbed
200g small raw
    peeled prawns
Alioli (page 308), to serve

Heat the olive oil in a 28–30cm cazuela or shallow flameproof casserole over medium heat. Add the shallot and fry gently for 5 minutes until soft. Add the garlic and fry for 40 to 60 seconds, then stir in the fish stock, parsley and salt and bring to the boil.

Sprinkle in the rice, stir once, then leave to simmer vigorously over medium-high heat for 6 minutes. Put the clams and prawns on top and shake the pan briefly so they sink into the rice a little. Lower the heat and leave to simmer gently for another 12 minutes. At the end of this time, almost all the liquid should be absorbed and the rice will be pitted with small holes. Serve with alioli.

MUSSEL PILAF *WITH* CINNAMON, CUMIN & SAFFRON

SERVES FOUR TO SIX

This must be the definitive seafood dish of Thessaloniki – it appears in every restaurant. I love the Greek way of cooking rice. This would have fitted well in my last book, *Venice to Istanbul*, where I often traced Byzantine food influences. Though this is a northern Greek dish, you could easily imagine it being available in the streets of eastern Turkey.

750g raw mussels, scrubbed
90ml olive oil
1 large onion, finely chopped
1 green pepper, seeded
    and finely chopped
2 cloves garlic, finely
    chopped or grated
Pinch saffron threads
½ tsp ground cinnamon
½ tsp ground cumin
½ tsp chilli flakes
Good handful dill,
    roughly chopped
1 tsp salt
2 medium tomatoes, skinned
    and finely chopped
Juice ½ lemon
400g long-grain rice

Put the mussels in a pan with a splash of water, cover and steam over high heat for about 3 to 4 minutes until open, shaking the pan from time to time. Pour the mussels into a colander set over a bowl. Remove the shells from all but 25 of them and set the cooked mussels aside. Pour all but the last (gritty) tablespoonful of mussel liquor into a measuring jug and top up with water to 800ml.

In a large pan over a medium heat, warm the olive oil, then gently fry the onion, green pepper, garlic and spices for about 10 minutes. Add half the dill with the salt, chopped tomato and lemon juice and cook for a couple of minutes. Add the rice and stir through.

Pour in the mussel stock and bring to the boil. Cover with a lid and simmer for 12 to 15 minutes or until the rice is soft. Add the cooked mussels and the rest of the dill and stir through.

DANISH FISH FRIKADELLER
WITH REMOULADE

=== SERVES FOUR ===

Right in the middle of the Tivoli Gardens in Copenhagen is the Grøften, a massive 600-seat restaurant which has been going since 1864. Its new chef, Jacob Elkjær, has bought his famous fish cakes from his home town of Middelfart. He says the secret is not to use too much flour or milk. I like Jacob, a very enthusiastic and successful restaurateur, and especially the fish cakes with his own remoulade sauce. Serve with new potatoes or Warm Potato Salad (page 296).

650g skinless boneless
 cod fillet
150ml whipping cream
Zest ½ lemon
1 egg, beaten
80g plain flour, plus
 extra for dusting
¾ tsp salt
12 turns black peppermill
Small handful dill, chopped
1 tbsp capers, chopped
40g butter

For the remoulade
120g *Mustard mayonnaise*
 (page 308)
2 tbsp finely chopped capers
2 tbsp finely chopped
 pickled gherkins
1 small onion, finely grated
Squeeze lemon juice
2 tsp Dijon mustard
¼ tsp curry powder
Small handful
 chives, chopped
3–4 sprigs fresh
 tarragon, chopped
3 tbsp whipping cream,
 lightly whipped

Combine the fish with the whipping cream, lemon zest, egg, flour, salt and pepper in a food processor and pulse until combined. Transfer to a bowl and stir in the chopped dill and capers. The mixture will be a bit sticky. With lightly floured hands divide into 8 to 12 portions – depending on what size you like your frikadeller – and form into flat patties. Heat the butter until foaming and fry the patties for 4 to 5 minutes on each side until golden. Keep warm.

Mix together all the ingredients for the remoulade, folding in the whipped cream at the end. Serve alongside the frikadeller.

PASTA CHI VRUOCCULI ARRIMINATI
SICILIAN PASTA WITH CAULIFLOWER, ANCHOVIES, CURRANTS & PINE NUTS

SERVES FOUR TO SIX

At the back of the Quattro Canti, the Baroque square in the centre of Palermo, there is a restaurant called Bisso Bistrot. It's informal, cheap and incredibly busy. You can't book but it's worth the wait. I ordered this dish of pasta with a sauce of cauliflower, which they call 'broccoli', just to see what could be made of something apparently so bland. They were far too busy to give me the recipe so this may not be quite the same, but either way what I had was delicious, particularly the pasta, which was daringly al dente.

350g cauliflower florets
Salt, for cooking
30g pine nuts
6 tbsp olive oil
50g dried white
   Breadcrumbs (page 309)
1 medium onion,
   finely chopped
6 anchovy fillets from a tin,
   drained and chopped
Large pinch chilli flakes
Pinch saffron threads
40g currants
½ tsp salt
5 turns black peppermill
400g dried spaghetti
Handful flat-leaf
   parsley, chopped

Cook the cauliflower florets in boiling salted water for 8 to 10 minutes until tender. Set aside, reserving the cooking water.

In a dry frying pan over a medium heat, toast the pine nuts for 1 to 2 minutes, shaking the pan often and taking care they don't catch and burn. Tip into a bowl and set aside. In the same pan, heat 3 tablespoons of the olive oil, add the breadcrumbs and fry for 4 to 5 minutes until crisp and golden. Set aside.

In a wide pan over medium heat, warm 2 tablespoons of the olive oil and fry the onion gently until soft, about 5 minutes. Add the anchovies and chilli flakes and continue to cook for 3 to 5 minutes or until the anchovies have almost disintegrated. Add the cauliflower florets, about 100ml cauliflower cooking water and the saffron and cook for 6 to 8 minutes. Mash the cauliflower with a potato masher or back of a wooden spoon to break it up to create a thick but loose sauce. Add the pine nuts, currants, salt and black pepper.

Cook the pasta in plenty of salted boiling water until al dente, following packet instructions. Drain well and add to the pan along with the remaining tablespoon of olive oil. Add a little more cauliflower water if the sauce is too thick to coat the pasta. Toss in half of the breadcrumb mixture and three-quarters of the chopped parsley. Stir well to combine.

Divide between serving bowls and top with the remaining breadcrumbs and parsley.

PRAWNS & CLAMS WITH GARLIC & CORIANDER

SERVES FOUR

Cervejaria Ramiro is a must-visit seafood restaurant in Lisbon. Most of the dishes are simply boiled crab or prawns, percebes or murex sea snails, but I was very keen to bring just one recipe from the restaurant because I liked the place so much. This is it, simple but so typical of wonderful Portuguese seafood cooking.

70ml olive oil
4 garlic cloves, crushed
1 piri-piri or bird's eye chilli
8 large raw prawns, shell on
20 raw clams, scrubbed
Juice ½ lemon
½ tsp salt
Small handful coriander, roughly chopped
Crusty bread, to serve

Heat the olive oil in a wide pan over medium heat. Add the garlic and chilli, and fry for 1 or 2 minutes until fragrant. Add the prawns and cook for 3 minutes, turning frequently.

Increase the heat to high and add the clams, turning them over as they open. Add the lemon juice and salt. Let the liquid reduce a little, then throw in the coriander and serve immediately with lots of crusty bread.

SIMPLE COD GRATIN
WITH BÉARNAISE SAUCE TOPPING
═ SERVES FOUR ═

This dish has Icelandic inspiration, though it's not something I actually ate in Reykjavik. The best things about this are the chunky carrots and leeks, the generous quantity of cod, and the Béarnaise sauce, which I added because I know how much the Icelanders love it. Tarragon and fish go so well together.

40g butter
2 leeks, sliced
1 onion, chopped
2 carrots, sliced
600g cod loin, skinned,
    cut into 3cm chunks
2 tbsp plain flour
50ml dry white wine
Salt and freshly ground
    black pepper

For the Béarnaise sauce
70ml white wine vinegar
2 shallots, finely chopped
2 sprigs fresh tarragon
1 bay leaf
6 peppercorns
4 egg yolks
300g unsalted butter
1 tsp fresh tarragon, chopped
Salt and freshly ground
    black pepper

Melt the butter in a saucepan over medium heat and sweat the leek, onion and carrot until softened and starting to caramelise, about 5 to 10 minutes. Add the cod and the flour, and stir for 1 to 2 minutes. Add the white wine and allow to thicken for 1 minute. Season with salt and pepper to taste. Spoon into a buttered oven dish and cover.

Heat the oven to 180°C/gas 4.

For the sauce, warm the vinegar in a saucepan over medium heat, and add the shallots, tarragon, bay leaf and peppercorns. Cook until the volume of liquid has reduced by more than half. Strain and set aside until completely cooled.

Bake the cod and vegetables for 15 to 20 minutes.

Meanwhile, beat the egg yolks with a teaspoon of water. Stir into the cooled vinegar. Pour the mixture into a bain-marie (a bowl set over a pan of simmering water) over a medium heat and whisk constantly until the sauce has thickened enough to coat the back of a spoon and has increased in volume.

Melt the unsalted butter.

Remove the bowl from the heat and slowly pour in the melted butter in a steady stream, whisking continuously, until the mixture has thickened and is smooth. Fold in the chopped tarragon and season, to taste, with salt and pepper.

Heat the grill to hot. Take the cod from the oven and pour the Béarnaise sauce over it. Flash under the hot grill for 3 to 4 minutes until nicely browned, and serve.

FENNEL & SAUSAGE RAGÙ
WITH TAGLIATELLE

=== SERVES FOUR ===

This is the sort of pasta dish I always seek out in Italian restaurants because I love fennel-flavoured sausages. At home, I find it's easier to reproduce the flavour by using good-quality sausagemeat and adding fennel seeds, chilli, garlic, rosemary, salt and black pepper. What I love about this dish is that it is nurtured with plenty of cream and served with homemade egg tagliatelle. Memories for me of Mercato delle Erbe, a market space energized by a couple of brilliant restaurants, Altro and, across the other side, a seafood grill, Banco32, where they make dishes from whatever fish is available on the counter.

400g coarse pork
   sausagemeat
1 tbsp olive oil
1 small onion, finely chopped
1 large clove garlic, grated
2 sticks celery, chopped
¾ tsp fennel seeds,
   roughly ground
¼ tsp chilli flakes
Sprig fresh rosemary,
   leaves finely chopped
1 tsp salt
12 turns black peppermill
150ml dry white wine
150ml double cream
150ml *Chicken stock*
   (page 307)

For the pasta dough
400g 00 pasta flour
4 eggs, lightly beaten
2 tsp salt
50g Parmesan cheese,
   freshly grated, to serve

Break up the sausagemeat into a large ovenproof pan and add half the oil to start with. If the sausagemeat is fatty, it might render quite a bit of lard and you won't need the rest of the olive oil; if it's quite dry, you will. Cook on medium heat for around 10 minutes, stirring from time to time, then add the onion, garlic, celery, fennel seeds, chilli, rosemary and salt and pepper, then cook for a further 15 minutes. Pour in the wine, cook for few minutes until reduced by half, then add the cream and chicken stock. Put a lid on the pan and simmer the mixture gently for half an hour.

In a food processor, combine the flour, eggs and salt, then tip on to a work surface and bring together in a ball of dough. Cover in clingfilm and rest for 20 to 30 minutes.

Roll out the pasta into a couple of sheets about 2mm thick. Run through a pasta machine, or use a knife or pizza cutter, to cut into 5mm-wide ribbons. Separate the strands and leave to dry on the back of a chair or spread out on a tray.

When ready to serve, cook the tagliatelle in plenty of boiling salted water for about 4 minutes until al dente. Drain and add to the ragù pan.

Combine the ragù with the pasta and serve in warmed bowls with freshly grated Parmesan.

SPAGHETTI ALLA BOLOGNESE

≡ SERVES FOUR ≡

If you want to wind up the people of Bologna, talk about spaghetti bolognese. You will be firmly told that tagliatelle is to be served with ragù bolognese, never spaghetti. Tagliatelle comes from Bologna, where it is made with good eggs and 00 flour, making a soft, malleable, silky pasta. Spaghetti comes from southern Italy, where they don't have many eggs but they can grow durum wheat, and where the pasta is made just with flour and water. However, I discovered that there is actually a spaghetti bolognese, which the locals cook of a Friday fish day, made with tomatoes, tuna and dry pasta. Monica Venturi, whose sister's recipe for tortelloni appears on page 289, cooked this for me in her lovely tidy flat overlooking the Mercato delle Erbe. It is astonishingly simple but I couldn't believe how good it was, especially served with a glass of Pignoletto Frizzante.

2 tbsp olive oil
1 large onion, sliced
400g tin plum tomatoes
1 tsp sugar
1 tsp salt
400g spaghetti
160g tuna flakes
    (drained weight)
40g Parmesan cheese cheese,
    freshly grated
Freshly ground black pepper

Heat the olive oil in a frying pan over medium heat and fry the onion until soft, about 5 to 10 minutes. Add the tomatoes, sugar and salt, and reduce the sauce a little to intensify the flavour.

Cook the spaghetti in plenty of boiling, salted water, following packet instructions. Drain well. Add the tuna flakes to the tomato sauce and stir through the pasta. Serve immediately with Parmesan and black pepper.

ICELANDIC BREADED LAMB CHOPS
WITH SPICED RED CABBAGE

=== SERVES EIGHT ===

I don't know why, but until I went to Iceland I had never considered cooking lamb chops in breadcrumbs. There it's almost the most common way of preparing them. This dish is particularly lovely when made with tender, best end chops. The lamb is gently cooked in clarified butter in a pan, and the essential accompaniment is a special spiced red cabbage, using fresh blueberries and bramble jelly as well as apple, onion, vinegar and sugar. Serve with boiled potatoes rolled in melted butter and sprinkled with chopped parsley.

For the lamb chops
8 large best end chops
Salt and freshly ground
    black pepper
Plain flour, for coating
2 eggs, beaten
100g dried white
    Breadcrumbs (page 309)
60g *Clarified butter*
    (page 309), for frying
2 tbsp vegetable/rapeseed oil

For the spiced red cabbage
1 large onion, sliced
60g butter
1 red cabbage (around
    750g–1kg), finely shredded
1 large Bramley apple,
    peeled, cored and chopped
50ml red wine vinegar
60g fresh blueberries
2 tbsp dark brown sugar
4 tbsp bramble jelly or jam,
    or redcurrant jelly
3 cloves
5cm cinnamon stick
1½ tsp salt
20 turns black peppermill
125ml water

First make the spiced cabbage. In a large saucepan over medium heat, sweat the onion in the butter for 5 to 10 minutes. Add the shredded cabbage, cook for 2 minutes, then add the apple, vinegar, blueberries, brown sugar, jelly or jam, cloves, cinnamon stick, salt, pepper and water. Cover with a well-fitting lid and cook until softened, about an hour. After 45 minutes, check the liquid and, if it is drying out, add a splash more. If there is a lot of liquid in the pan, remove the lid and evaporate off the excess. Remove the cinnamon stick and cloves before serving.

Season the chops with salt and pepper. Toss in plain flour, then dip in beaten egg and finish by coating all over with breadcrumbs. Heat the butter and oil in a large frying pan until hot, then fry the chops until golden all over and cooked through, about 7 to 8 minutes per side.

CHICKPEA WITH CHORIZO TAPAS

Dishes like this are the mainstay of tapas bars. When I walked into Francisco Jimenez aka Pancho's kitchen in Ultramar & Nos, a modern tapas bar in Cadiz, he had three stews going on the stove: this one, a similar one with a different type of chorizo and pinto beans, and one of dogfish tuna and potatoes. All were his mother's recipes, and all were very good, but I marginally preferred this one because it had more chorizo in it. Just for the record, I also ordered *jamón ibérico* ham, white anchovies and tuna escabeche.

75ml olive oil
1 medium onion, chopped
2 cloves garlic, grated
    or finely chopped
150g chorizo sausage, diced
1 small red pepper,
    seeded and chopped
1 small green pepper,
    seeded and chopped
2 bay leaves
90ml red wine
1½ tsp hot smoked paprika
    (*pimentón picante*)
2 x 400g tins
    chickpeas, drained
    (480g drained weight)
¾ tsp salt
8 turns black peppermill
Small handful flat-leaf
    parsley, chopped

In a medium saucepan over a low heat, warm 50ml of the olive oil and sweat the onion and garlic for 3 to 5 minutes until starting to soften. Add the chorizo, peppers and bay leaves, and cook for a further 5 minutes until the orange fat starts to run from the sausage.

Add the red wine and paprika, increase the heat and reduce the liquid until it is just a loose coating sauce, 1 to 2 minutes.

Add the chickpeas, cover the pan, reduce the heat a little and cook for 3 to 4 minutes to warm them through. Season with the salt and pepper. Serve drizzled with the remaining olive oil and sprinkled with the parsley.

POLLO ALLA MARSALA
CHICKEN WITH MARSALA
SERVES FOUR

Chicken Marsala was ubiquitous in the 1960s and 1970s. After that it lost its appeal but now, just as with the prawn cocktail, it is time for a revival. It's a beautiful dish, made more often in Sicily with veal but also found with chicken. What I particularly like about Italian meals is that by the time you get to the *terzo* course, all you want is a small piece of protein, such as chicken, fish or steak, and maybe a salad and a couple of sauté potatoes. *Recipe photograph overleaf*

4 skinless, boneless
   chicken breasts
Salt and freshly ground
   black pepper
40g plain flour
50g butter
2 tbsp olive oil
2 shallots, finely chopped
1 clove garlic,
   finely chopped
160g chestnut
   mushrooms, sliced
250ml dry Marsala
150ml *Chicken stock*
   (page 307)
Sauté potatoes
   (page 308), to serve
Small handful flat-leaf
   parsley, chopped

Place the chicken breasts between sheets of clingfilm and beat, using a meat mallet or rolling pin, until about 5mm thick. Season with salt and pepper on both sides, then dip in the plain flour to coat lightly, shaking off any excess. Melt half the butter with 1 tablespoon of the olive oil in a frying pan over medium-high heat and fry the chicken for 2 to 3 minutes per side until golden. Set aside.

Wipe out the pan with kitchen paper. Heat the remaining butter and olive oil over medium heat and gently fry the shallot and garlic for about 5 minutes until softened. Add the mushrooms and cook for 2 minutes, then add the Marsala and turn the heat up to high. Reduce the liquid by about half. Turn the heat back down, add the chicken stock and chicken, and cook the chicken in the sauce for about 10 minutes. Serve with sauté potatoes sprinkled with parsley.

KOZANI CHICKEN *WITH* PRUNES, SAFFRON & PAPRIKA

Kozani is a town in Greek Macedonia, about an hour west of Thessaloniki, famous for its saffron. This chicken dish is popular in Thessaloniki too. It seems Byzantine in its influences: prunes, saffron, paprika. Serve with pilaf rice (page 308).

8 skinless chicken thighs
1 litre water
Pinch of Kozani or
    Spanish saffron
4 tbsp olive oil
3 red onions, finely sliced
1½ tbsp sweet paprika
20 pitted prunes
1 tsp salt
6 turns black peppermill

Put the chicken thighs in a large saucepan with the water and the saffron. Bring to the boil, then turn down the heat and allow to poach for 10 to 15 minutes. Drain, reserving the cooking liquid.

Heat the olive oil in a large saucepan over medium-low heat and sweat the onion gently until very soft, about 10 minutes. Add the paprika, cook for 2 minutes, then add the chicken thighs, about 700ml of the cooking liquid and the prunes. Season with the salt and pepper and simmer for about 20 minutes, until heated through.

Check the pan with the chicken, and if it is very watery, remove the chicken, prunes and onions with a slotted spoon and keep warm while you reduce down the sauce, so that you have a small amount to spoon over each portion.

SATURDAY BRUNCH & LUNCH

A FRENCH HAMBURGER WITH CAMEMBERT OF COURSE 54

ICELANDIC LANGOUSTINE SOUP 57

WAFFLES & RHUBARB JAM 58

SOLLA'S VEGAN LASAGNE 60

CRISP PORK & BEEF PIE WITH ONIONS, RED PEPPER & OREGANO 61

MEATBALLS IN TOMATO SAUCE WITH CINNAMON & CUMIN 64

OEUFS EN COCOTTE WITH HAM & MUSHROOMS 66

SALT COD & CHIPS 67

A GRUYERE GRATIN OF CHICKEN, TOMATO & BLACK OLIVES 70

CONSTANTINOPLE-STYLE ARTICHOKE STEW 71

CHICKEN PIRI-PIRI 74

MACKEREL WITH PIRIÑACA SALAD 79

PORK & CLAMS ALENTEJO STYLE 80

FLAMENCO EGGS WITH TOMATO & SERRANO HAM 82

ROCKET SALAD WITH FIGS, PARMA HAM, GORGONZOLA & BASIL 85

INVOLTINI DI PESCE SPADA 88

RAVIOLI WITH PORCINI MUSHROOMS, SUN-DRIED TOMATOES & HAZELNUTS 89

PORTUGUESE BREAD STEW WITH PRAWNS 92

METEOR SHOWER 93

ARANCINI SALSICCIA 96

In the 1970s and 1980s my first wife, Jill, and I used to close the restaurant at the end of September and not reopen again until late March, just before Easter. During those winter months we lived rather an idyllic life. We travelled a lot, first on our own and then with our young family, to places like Thailand, India and Australia, and we used to invite our friends down for long weekend house parties. In those days I used my friends as testers for my recipes and I would make things like puff pastry and croissants early on Saturday morning for their late breakfast, which became more of a brunch. I even had a try at making baguettes from Julia Child and Simone Beck's *Mastering the Art of French Cooking*, whose many pages of instructions didn't emphasize the fact that it's not possible to make them successfully without a) French bread flour and b) a steam-injection soleplate baker's oven. Everyone was always very complimentary, notably my sister Henrietta and my brother-in-law Philip Davis, and our friends Richard and Pattie Barber. The house, a large Victorian one on Trevose Head near Padstow, had a lovely big kitchen warmed by an Aga and, something I have always missed since, a larder/pantry. On those weekends, nobody made it downstairs until about ten o'clock in the morning so, in addition to the not-quite-perfect croissants and bread, I'd knock up a corned beef hash or baked egg dish, like the Huevos a la Flamenca on page 82, or something sweet like the Waffles and Rhubarb Jam on page 58.

Brunch soon runs into Saturday lunch, a time to enjoy some slightly daring cooking. If you think of the weekend as a sort of sine wave, this time on a Saturday you are definitely on the way up. Time for some perky and unusual wines and food. The Pork and Clams Alentejo-style (page 80) springs to mind; anyone who's been to the Algarve or Alentejo in southern Portugal will have had it. The pork is marinated in roasted and pounded red peppers, sea salt and olive oil, then quickly fried with the clams with garlic, white wine and smoked paprika. It's crying out for a glass or two of Vinho Verde. Or the gigantic Bologna Salad (page 85), where I've taken most of the leaves from a good vegetable stall in a market and mixed them with whatever sweet fruits I can get hold of – figs, peaches, you could even use pears – and Parma ham, Parmesan, tomatoes and some luxurious cheese like Gorgonzola Dolce. Add a pile of sourdough bread (page 120), and maybe a plate of grilled sardines and a bottle or two of crisp white wine like Txakolí from San Sebastián or Picpoul de Pinet from the Languedoc, for the perfect, informal, exuberant Saturday lunch.

A FRENCH HAMBURGER
WITH CAMEMBERT OF COURSE

SERVES FOUR

As in the UK, rents in prosperous cities like Bordeaux are often too high for young entrepreneurial chefs and restaurateurs, who have responded by doing pop-ups or taking to the road in a van. In Bordeaux you can eat and drink very well from these. I was particularly struck by the burger van, as the guy who ran it, Ben Lethbridge, seemed so cheerful and enthusiastic, and I was much struck by a burger with Camembert as a cheese rather than Monterey Jack. The combination is theirs, but the patty recipe is one we use in our pub, the Cornish Arms in St Merryn. Ideally get your butcher to coarsely mince the chuck steak and fat together; you need the mixture to be about 15 per cent fat. This combination of meat and fat seasoned with salt and pepper is all you need, no fillers or binding agents. The mustard mayo is used in our Seafood Restaurant in Padstow, usually with English mustard, and is delicious. Store whatever is left in a jar in the fridge for up to a week and use in sandwiches and coleslaw. Serve the burgers with mustard mayo coleslaw or French fries.

1 tbsp sunflower oil,
    plus extra for cooking
    the burgers
2 onions, finely sliced
500g chuck steak, coarsely
    minced with 75g beef fat
7g salt
5g freshly ground
    black pepper
4 burger buns, cut
    through the middle
100g Camembert cheese,
    sliced
1 beefsteak tomato, sliced
Salad leaves
Mustard mayonnaise
    (page 308), to serve

Make the mustard mayo in a food processor. Start by adding the egg yolks to the bowl with the white wine vinegar, salt and mustard, and blend for a few seconds. With the motor still running, carefully add the sunflower oil in a thin and steady stream. The mayo will gradually thicken. When all the oil is incorporated, check the consistency. If too thick, add a teaspoon or two of cold water with the motor still running. Check seasoning and store in a jar in the fridge until needed.

In a pan over medium heat, warm the sunflower oil and cook the onion until softened, 5 to 10 minutes, then raise the heat slightly to lightly brown them. Keep warm until ready to serve.

Mix the meat with the salt and pepper. Divide the mixture into four balls, and flatten to form a burger patty.

Heat a frying pan or griddle pan until hot, drizzle with a little sunflower oil and fry the burgers until cooked to the desired state – a meat probe is best for this. For medium, cook 6 to 7 minutes each side to an internal temp of 55°C; for well done, cook at least 8 minutes each side to an internal temperature over 70°C. When ready, set aside, while you toast the cut sides of the buns in the pan.

Assemble the burgers: dollop some mustard mayo on the bottom bun, top with a burger, a couple of slices of Camembert, then the fried onions, the tomato slice and the salad leaves.

ICELANDIC LANGOUSTINE SOUP

═ SERVES FOUR ═

I was in two minds whether to include this recipe in the book because for complete success you have to be able to get hold of very good quality langoustines, and they are neither easy to come by nor cheap, not unless you live on the west coast of Scotland or Ireland. However, what won the day was that it is a soup of such deliciousness. The recipe comes from a restaurant called Fjöruborðið in Stokkseyri about 36 miles from Reykjavik, where they serve more or less nothing else. You can either have the soup on its own or as a first course with the tails fried in butter afterwards. The restaurant is packed every day; it's a bit like the Icelandic version of the Crab House in Florida.

8 large cooked langoustines
  in the shell
100g butter
1 large white onion, chopped
1 large carrot, chopped
2 sticks celery, chopped
1½ litres *Fish stock* (page 307)
50ml white wine
1 tsp curry powder
2 medium red peppers,
  deseeded and sliced
1 medium tomato, skinned,
  roughly chopped
2 tsp tomato paste
½ tsp red Tabasco
200ml double cream
½–1 tsp salt, to taste

Remove the langoustine tails from the shells and set aside. Crush the shells by rolling them with a rolling pin on a chopping board. Heat half the butter in a large pan, add the shells, half the onion and all the carrot and celery. Fry over medium-high heat, stirring constantly, for 5 minutes, then add the fish stock and wine, bring to the boil and simmer very gently for an hour. Pass through a strainer.

Heat the remaining butter in a large pan over medium heat and add the curry powder, the rest of the onion and the red pepper, and cook gently until soft, about 5 to 10 minutes. Add the tomato and tomato paste, the strained stock and Tabasco, bring to the boil, then simmer for 15 minutes.

Liquidize the soup in a processor or blender, return to the pan, add the cream and simmer for another 5 minutes. Put the reserved langoustine tails into the soup to warm through for a minute or two.

Correct the seasoning with salt and pour the soup into the soup bowls, ensuring everyone gets 2 langoustine tails.

WAFFLES *AND* RHUBARB JAM

MAKES EIGHT TO TEN WAFFLES

I had to include this recipe from Reykjavik in honour of Mayor Dagur Bergþóruson Eggertsson, who invited me round for waffles. He has an open day once a year when anyone can go. He had a lovely house, all painted tongue-and-groove panelling, and a dresser stuffed full of sensible glasses, big coffee cups, casseroles and thick, rugged-looking plates. The rhubarb jam will fill four to five 340g jars.

For the waffles
300g plain flour
1 tbsp baking powder
1 tbsp caster sugar
Pinch salt
2 large eggs, beaten
400ml full-fat milk
1 tsp vanilla extract
90g butter, melted

For the rhubarb jam
1kg cleaned, trimmed
    rhubarb, cut into
    3cm lengths
1kg granulated sugar
1 sachet (8g) pectin
    OR use 1kg jam sugar in
    place of sugar and pectin
Juice 1 large lemon
5 x 340g jam jars

For the jam, combine the rhubarb with the sugar and pectin in a large jam pan and mix well to coat the rhubarb in the sugar. Leave for 4 hours or overnight to allow the juices to run.

Add the lemon juice to the rhubarb and sugar and set the pan over low heat to start with to allow the sugar to dissolve. Once the sugar is liquid, increase the temperature and bring up to the boil. Put a couple of saucers in the freezer. Boil the jam for 20 to 30 minutes, then test for setting point by putting a teaspoonful on a cold saucer and allowing to cool for a minute. Push it with your finger: if it wrinkles, it is ready; if not, give the jam a few more minutes. Check every 3 to 5 minutes, taking care not to burn the jam. Alternatively, use a sugar thermometer to test when it has reached 103–105°C. This jam is better a bit soft rather than too stiff.

When the jam is ready, use a jam funnel and a ladle to fill the jars. Cover the jam with a disc of waxed paper and put the lids on. When cool, label and store in a cool, dark place.

For the waffles, sift the dry ingredients into a mixing bowl. Beat the eggs into the milk and stir in the vanilla. Gradually whisk the milk mixture into the flour mixture. Finally, stir in the melted butter. Rest the batter for 5 minutes while you heat the waffle iron, and grease it if necessary.

Add a ladleful of batter to the hot iron. Cook until browned and crisp (this will depend on your waffle iron and heat setting). Keep warm on baking sheets in a low oven (about 110°C/gas ¼) to keep crisp until you have used all the batter. Serve warm with rhubarb jam.

SOLLA'S VEGAN LASAGNE

═ SERVES THREE TO FOUR ═

Solveig Eiríksdóttir, better known as Solla, is famous in Iceland for being a champion of raw food. I have to own up to some incredulity when I heard about 'raw lasagne', but then I went to Solla's house and watched her prepare this extraordinary dish with a growing sense of admiration. Solla absolutely knows what she is doing. There is no question of losing satisfying flavours. Nutritional yeast and onion powder, plus sensible seasoning, give everything umami. Incidentally, just at the end she said it would also be great baked in the oven!

2 courgettes
1 large avocado
Lemon juice

For the nut cheese
70g Brazil nuts, soaked
    in water for 2 hours
70g cashew nuts, soaked
    in water for 2 hours
2–3 tbsp water
2 tbsp lemon juice
2 tbsp nutritional yeast
1 tsp probiotic powder
1 tsp onion powder
½ tsp sea salt
10 turns black peppermill

For the green pesto
Large handful fresh basil (30g)
Large handful of rocket (30g)
70g cashew nuts
2 tbsp nutritional yeast
1 large clove garlic, peeled
¼–½ tsp sea salt flakes
60ml cold-pressed olive oil

For the red pesto
125g sun-dried tomatoes
1 clove garlic, peeled
2 plum tomatoes,
    roughly chopped
20g dates, pitted and soaked
    in a cup of boiling water
    for 5 minutes, drained
½ red pepper, deseeded
1 red chilli, deseeded
1 tsp oregano
1 tbsp water
¼ tsp sea salt flakes

For the nut cheese, put everything in a food processor and pulse to make a coarse paste.

For each pesto, put all the ingredients in a food processor and blend to a rough paste.

To assemble the lasagne, slice the courgettes very finely lengthways on a mandolin or with a sharp knife. Peel, stone and slice the avocado thinly, then coat in lemon juice. On each plate lay a couple of slices of courgette, then a few slices of avocado, a dollop of red pesto, then green pesto, a layer of nut cheese, then a layer of courgette. Repeat, ending with the nut cheese.

The lasagne is intended to be eaten raw, but could be assembled in an ovenproof dish and baked for 15 to 20 minutes at 180°C/gas 4, drizzled with a little olive oil.

KIMA BOUGATSA
CRISP PORK & BEEF PIE *WITH* ONIONS, RED PEPPER & OREGANO

=== MAKES TWELVE SQUARES ===

Next time I'm in Thessaloniki I must go to Bantis Bougatsa for their savoury bougatsa – a crisp filo parcel of minced buffalo meat with chopped onions, garlic, cumin and olive oil. The filo layers are brushed with sheep's milk butter, which smells like Indian ghee. The shop opens at 5 a.m. and you can buy bougatsa straight from the oven, which is very heart warming if you're up early or going to bed late. My version is just a little different, taking into account the lack of availability in the UK of minced buffalo meat and sheep's milk butter. *Recipe photograph overleaf*

4 tbsp olive oil
4 medium onions, chopped
1 red pepper, finely chopped
150g minced pork
150g minced beef
¼ tsp chilli flakes
2 tsp dried oregano
2 tbsp tomato paste
200ml *Chicken stock*
   (page 307)
½ tsp salt
10 turns black peppermill
12 large sheets filo pastry
   (250g pack)
130g butter, melted

Heat the oil in a large, wide frying pan over medium heat and gently fry the onion and red pepper until soft, about 10 minutes. Add the pork and beef and continue to fry for another 10 minutes, stirring frequently. Add the chilli flakes, oregano, tomato paste and stock, and season with the salt and pepper. Continue to cook for about another 10 minutes until most of the liquid has evaporated. Set aside to cool.

Heat the oven to 190°C/gas 5.

Using a large baking tray about 40cm x 30cm and 3cm deep, lay a sheet of filo in the base. Brush with melted butter. Repeat with another 5 sheets. Spread the filling over the filo. Lay another sheet of filo over the filling, and use up the remaining sheets, buttering between each layer. Finish by buttering the top.

Bake for 25 to 30 minutes until golden brown and crisp. Allow to sit for 5 to 10 minutes before cutting into 12 squares or diamonds. Serve while still warm.

SOUTZOUKAKIA
MEATBALLS IN TOMATO SAUCE
WITH CINNAMON & CUMIN

=== SERVES FOUR ===

If you love meatballs in tomato sauce as much as I do, you'll find these are particularly special. Indeed, I would say they are almost the signature dish of Thessaloniki. There is probably not a traditional restaurant that doesn't serve them. My recipe is an amalgamation of all the ones I have had. Interestingly, most restaurants do the same *soutzoukakia* simply grilled over charcoal and served with sliced red onions and often skordalia (see page 67), which is very good too. Serve this with rice garnished with twelve green olives.

For the meatballs
500g minced beef
2 cloves garlic, finely
    chopped or grated
1 egg, beaten
½ tsp ground cumin
½ tsp dried oregano
2 slices stale white bread
    (about 100g), soaked in
    red wine and squeezed dry
½ tsp salt
12 turns black peppermill
3 tbsp olive oil

For the tomato sauce
1 onion, finely chopped
1 clove garlic, finely chopped
3 tbsp olive oil
5cm cinnamon stick
1 tsp ground cumin
1 tsp sugar
150ml red wine
1 tbsp tomato paste
500ml passata
½ tsp salt
12 turns black peppermill

Mix together all the ingredients for the meatballs except the olive oil and, with wet hands, shape into 20 to 24 rugby-ball shapes. Heat the oil in a frying pan over high heat and fry the meatballs until golden on all sides, or grill on a griddle pan if you like grill lines on the patties.

Make the tomato sauce by sweating the onion and garlic in the olive oil with the cinnamon stick, cumin and sugar until soft, about 10 minutes over medium heat. Add the red wine and bring to the boil, then reduce the heat to medium again. Add the tomato paste and passata, season with the salt and pepper and cook until slightly thickened, about 20 minutes.

Add the fried meatballs and simmer for 20 to 30 minutes with a lid on the pan until cooked through, adding a little water if the sauce is too thick.

OEUFS EN COCOTTE
WITH HAM & MUSHROOMS

=== SERVES SIX ===

The idea for this recipe came from a little restaurant near the central market in Bordeaux. A note from our associate producer, Arezoo Farahzad, says, 'A grumpy chef and grumpy waiter make for disappointing food.' However, I often use a disappointing version of a much-loved dish to ask the question, how could I make it better? It concentrates the mind. I'm very happy with this. I think it's an entirely Gallic way of enjoying the luxuriousness of good eggs.

30g butter
1 small onion, finely chopped
1 small clove garlic, grated
3 portobello mushrooms, chopped
6 slices Bayonne, prosciutto or Parma ham, chopped
½ tsp salt
6 turns black peppermill, plus extra
6 eggs
12 tsp double cream (60ml)

To serve
1 tsp chopped parsley
Crusty bread

Heat the oven to 200°C/gas 6. Use about a third of the butter to grease 6 ramekin dishes.

Melt the remaining butter in a pan over medium-low heat and soften the onion and garlic for a few minutes. Add the mushrooms and ham and continue to cook until the moisture from the mushrooms has evaporated. Season with the salt and pepper.

Spoon the ham and mushrooms into the ramekins and break an egg on top of each one. Spoon 2 teaspoons of double cream over each one, and grind over a little black pepper. Set the ramekins in a deep roasting tin and pour in boiling water to come about halfway up the sides. Bake for 15 minutes until the whites are set but the yolks are still runny. Sprinkle each with a pinch of chopped parsley and serve immediately with crusty bread.

BAKALIAROS TIGANITOS
SALT COD AND CHIPS
═ SERVES FOUR ═

I am fed up with eating fish and chips in countries that offer our national dish as a way of attracting British people into their restaurants. Our food may be simple but there is a subtlety of detail which others don't always notice, such as the quality of the cod, the batter, and the frying medium, which for me must always be dripping. So when I saw this restaurant in Thessaloniki with its garish neon sign, I thought to give it a miss, but then I translated the word *bakaliaros* and realized that they were not using fresh fish but salt cod. And it wasn't any old salt cod, it was the best and moistest thick fillets from the centre of the loin. Not only that, they accompanied it with fried potato discs and easily my favourite sauce in Greece, skordalia. My wife Sas and I were in heaven. *Recipe photograph overleaf*

675g salt cod
1kg waxy potatoes
1 litre sunflower oil, for frying
250g self-raising flour
350–375ml cold water
5 turns black peppermill
4 lemon wedges, to serve

For the skordalia
1 chunky slice sourdough
    bread, crusts removed
50ml water
1–1½ tbsp red wine vinegar
40g walnuts
4 cloves garlic, grated
80ml olive oil
Pinch salt

Soak the salt cod in plenty of cold water for 24 to 48 hours, changing the water every 8 hours. How long it needs to soak depends on thickness and how salty and dry it is. Drain, pat dry with kitchen towel and cut into 4 even-sized pieces.

Peel the potatoes and slice about 3–5mm thick. Rinse in cold water and lay out to dry on a clean tea towel.

Make the skordalia. Soak the bread in the water mixed with 1 tablespoon of the vinegar for about 30 minutes. Squeeze out the excess water.

Pound the walnuts with a pestle and mortar. Add the garlic and the soaked bread and pound some more. Gradually incorporate the olive oil and season with the salt and a little more vinegar if required.

Heat the oil in a heavy-based pan to 130°C, using a probe or sugar thermometer to check. Fry the potato slices for about 7 to 8 minutes until part cooked but not coloured. Remove with a slotted spoon, drain on kitchen paper and set aside. Keep the oil in the pan.

Put the flour in a large bowl and whisk in enough cold water – start with 350ml – to make a thick batter that will stick to the fish. Season with pepper but no salt.

Heat the oil to 180°C and refry the chips for 4 to 5 minutes until golden. Remove with a slotted spoon and keep warm in an oven while you finish the fish. Increase the heat of the oil to 190°C. Dip the salt cod pieces into the batter and fry until crisp and golden, about 5 minutes. Serve immediately with the lemon wedges, the chips and a bowl of skordalia.

POULET AU PARMENTIER
A GRUYÈRE GRATIN OF CHICKEN
WITH TOMATO & BLACK OLIVES

══ SERVES SIX ══

This recipe comes from Chez Mémé in the village of Saint-Julien-Beychevelle in the Haut-Médoc on the left bank of the Gironde. The other customers were pretty upmarket for a village restaurant. Hardly surprising, I suppose, because villages like Saint-Julien, though beautiful, are almost ancillary to the great chateaux. At the largest table in the room were wine *négociants* from Bordeaux, hosted by Lily Barton, owner of Château Léoville Barton, who I first met years ago in the private dining room of London wine merchants Corney & Barrow, along with her late father. Also in the room were a group of Saudi Arabian dignitaries, keen that we make a food series in their country. On the back burner, I think.

30g butter
6 large or 8 small banana
    shallots, peeled and halved
3 carrots, chopped
2 sticks celery, chopped
1 clove garlic, finely chopped
4 tbsp white wine (60ml)
4 large ripe tomatoes, skinned
    and chopped, or 400g tin
    chopped plum tomatoes
1 tbsp tomato paste
350ml *Chicken stock*
    (page 307)
600g cooked chicken meat
    (from a roast or rotisserie
    chicken), shredded
16 black olives, halved
2 tbsp chopped parsley
Salt and freshly ground
    black pepper
50g Gruyère cheese

For the potato topping
1.5kg floury potatoes, such
    as King Edwards, peeled,
    cut into chunks
30g butter
5 tbsp double cream (75ml)
2 egg yolks
Salt and freshly ground
    black pepper

Boil the potatoes for the topping in salted water until tender, about 15 minutes.

Heat the butter in a saucepan over medium heat and sweat the shallot halves, carrots, celery and garlic until soft, 10 to 15 minutes. Add the white wine and cook for 1 minute, then add the tomatoes and tomato paste and the chicken stock, and cook for 10 to 15 minutes until reduced and thickened. Add the cooked chicken to the sauce, together with the olives and the chopped parsley, and season to taste with salt and pepper.

Drain the potatoes and rice them with a potato ricer or masher into a bowl. Add the butter, cream, egg yolks and seasoning.

Heat the oven to 180°C/gas 4.

Place the filling in an ovenproof dish about 20cm x 30cm, top with the mashed potato and grate over the Gruyère. Bake for 30 to 35 minutes until hot through and the potatoes are starting to turn golden.

CONSTANTINOPLE-STYLE ARTICHOKE STEW

SERVES FOUR TO SIX

The idea for this dish comes from a famous tripe restaurant in Thessaloniki called Tsarouchas. I went there to try their legendary tripe stew, but the display of warm food in trays in the front window reminded me of my trips in the 1970s and I also had to have a plate of artichoke stew with carrots, peas and celery, made memorable by large quantities of fresh dill stewed with them. *Recipe photograph overleaf*

6 tbsp olive oil
1 medium onion,
    finely chopped
4 sticks celery, sliced
16 small shallots,
    peeled but left whole
3 carrots, sliced into
    thick rounds
½ tsp salt
12 turns black peppermill
Juice ½ large lemon
500ml *Vegetable* or
    Chicken stock (page 307)
8 fresh artichoke hearts
    (prepared as on page 209)
    or 10–12 small new season
    artichokes, halved
4 medium waxy potatoes,
    peeled and cut into
    2cm-thick slices
Large handful fresh dill,
    roughly chopped
100g fresh or frozen peas

Heat half the olive oil in a large pan over medium heat. Add the onion, celery and whole shallots and sweat for about 5 minutes until starting to soften.

Add the carrots and season with the salt and pepper and lemon juice, then pour in the stock. Cover and cook for 15 minutes.

Add the artichoke hearts, potato slices and dill. Bring up to the boil then immediately turn down to a simmer. Cover and cook for 35 minutes. Add the peas and cook for a further 10 minutes. Check periodically that the liquid is not evaporating entirely. It should be absorbed but a little should remain, so top up with a splash of water if necessary.

Check seasoning and add more salt and pepper if required. Serve warm or cold, with the remaining olive oil drizzled over.

CHICKEN PIRI-PIRI

SERVES FOUR TO SIX

Dried piri-piri (African bird's eye) chillies are getting easier to come by, although you could get away with using other bird's eye chillies. On the Scoville scale they are under Scotch bonnets, i.e. about eight or nine out of ten. Chicken piri-piri, a Mozambican dish, is now synonymous with Portuguese cooking but so often the heat is hardly there at all. If you are going to call something 'piri-piri', make it hot! You find this dish all over Lisbon. I particularly recall Casa da India, where Sas and I stopped in for a beer and looked longingly at the piri-piri chicken on a charcoal grill in the window. 'I wish we were eating here,' she said prophetically. 'This looks just our sort of place.' Serve the chicken with salads and chips or potatoes.

1 x 1.5kg chicken, jointed into 8 pieces, or 8 large chicken thighs
1 lemon cut into wedges, to serve

For the marinade
2 tsp salt
2 cloves garlic, crushed or grated
Juice ½ lemon
2 tbsp olive oil

For the piri-piri sauce
7–8 dried piri-piri chillies, or 5–6 red jalapeño and 1 red bird's eye, roughly chopped, seeds left in
1 clove garlic, roughly chopped
1½ tbsp red wine vinegar or juice 1 lemon
125ml olive oil
1½ tbsp smoked hot paprika
½ tsp salt
¼ tsp caster sugar
1 tsp dried oregano

Mix all the marinade ingredients together in a bowl. Add the chicken pieces, coat well, then cover and leave for an hour in the fridge.

Make the piri-piri sauce by combining all the ingredients except the oregano to a paste in a food processor. Stir in the oregano at the end. If the sauce is too thick, let it down with a little more olive oil. This will keep in a sterilized glass jar in the fridge for a couple of weeks.

Heat the oven to 200°C/gas 6.

Put the marinated chicken pieces on a baking tray and roast for about 25 minutes; meanwhile, heat the grill to hot. Finish the chicken off under the hot grill for 5 minutes to crisp up the skin, then brush with about 4 tablespoons of the piri-piri sauce.

Alternatively, cook the chicken on a barbecue for about 15 minutes, skin-side down to crisp and slightly char it, then turn over and continue to cook for about 10 minutes or until cooked through. The chicken is ready when the internal temperature reaches 75°C. Brush with the piri-piri sauce as above.

Serve with lemon wedges and more of the piri-piri sauce on the side.

MACKEREL WITH PIRIÑACA SALAD

Next time you are in Cornwall wondering what to do with the string full of mackerel you have just caught, consider cooking them on a barbecue and serving them with new potatoes and *piriñaca*, which is part salad, part salsa, part sauce.

4 mackerel, gutted
Salt and freshly ground
    black pepper
Olive oil, for drizzing

For the piriñaca
6 ripe tomatoes, chopped
    into 1–2cm dice
1 green pepper, deseeded,
    finely chopped into
    1–2cm dice
½ mild onion, finely
    chopped into 1–2cm dice
2 tbsp extra-virgin olive oil
1 tbsp sherry vinegar
½ tsp salt

Mix the *piriñaca* ingredients and leave to marinate at room temperature for 30 minutes.

To barbecue the mackerel, slash the skin 2 or 3 times on the diagonal, season with salt and pepper and drizzle with olive oil. Cook for 3 to 5 minutes per side, then serve at once with the *piriñaca*.

PORK *AND* CLAMS ALENTEJO-STYLE

I had to have the pork and clams at João do Grão. On TripAdvisor it is one of those places that people love or hate; in my opinion, usually a sign of a good restaurant. The only thing I remember from first visiting Portugal in the 1960s was their skill at frying small pieces of pork coated in the most deliciously salty, savoury ingredients, mixed with succulent clams still in their shells and the smell of white wine. At João do Grão I was in heaven. True to character, they refused to be filmed.

For the massa de pimentão
6 large red peppers, deseeded
2 tbsp sea salt flakes
275ml olive oil

For the main dish
1kg pork fillet (tenderloin),
    in 3cm chunks
2 tbsp *massa de pimentão*
3 cloves garlic, grated
    or finely chopped
1½ tsp hot smoked paprika
    (*pimentón picante*)
300ml dry white wine
75ml olive oil
1 onion, chopped
1 tsp tomato paste
800g raw clams, scrubbed
Salt and freshly ground
    black pepper
Handful coriander, chopped

Make the *massa de pimentão* in advance; it will keep for a couple of weeks in the fridge or can be frozen. Cut the peppers into strips and layer them in a glass bowl, alternating with the salt. Cover with clingfilm and leave for 24 hours at room temperature.

Heat the oven to 150°C/gas 2. Drain the peppers, put them on a baking sheet and slow-roast for about 1½ hours. Transfer to a bowl, cover and allow to cool slightly. Slip the skin off, then process the peppers to a paste in a food processor. Add the olive oil and store in a glass jar until ready to use.

Put the pork chunks in a bowl. Add the *massa de pimentão*, garlic and paprika and massage into the meat. Pour in the white wine. Transfer to the fridge and chill for at least 12 and up to 24 hours.

Strain the marinated pork through a sieve or colander over a bowl and reserve the marinade. Heat 2 to 3 tablespoons of the oil in a large, shallow flameproof casserole with a lid. Fry the pork in batches over a high heat until browned all over.

Reduce the heat to medium. Return all the pork to the pan along with the rest of the olive oil and the onion and fry until the onion starts to soften, 4 to 5 minutes. Stir in the tomato paste and the reserved marinade, turn up the heat slightly to medium-high and bring to the boil. Continue to cook for a couple of minutes to reduce the liquid by half, then add the clams to the pan. Cover with a lid and allow the clams to steam open, 3 to 5 minutes.

Taste the liquid and season to taste with salt and pepper. Stir through three-quarters of the coriander, scatter with the remainder and serve at once.

HUEVOS A LA FLAMENCA
FLAMENCO EGGS WITH TOMATO & SERRANO HAM

SERVES FOUR

This what you might call Spain on a plate, a sum-up dish of everything we love about Spanish cooking: serrano ham, chorizo, *pimentón*, tomatoes, garlic and onion. To these basic ingredients I have added green beans and peas; you could also add sliced, cooked new potatoes or chickpeas or the big butter beans called *judión*. Actually I first tried this in Cadiz and wasn't particularly knocked out by it, but I love eggs with tomato sauce, so I did a bit of research and came up with my own version.

4 tbsp olive oil
1 small onion, chopped
1 clove garlic, chopped
80g serrano ham, chopped
1 tsp hot smoked paprika
    (*pimentón picante*)
8 large tomatoes
    (about 750g), skinned and
    chopped, or 2 x 400g tins
    of peeled plum tomatoes
1 tsp tomato paste
75g peas, fresh or frozen
100g fine green beans
4 eggs
12 slices chorizo sausage
1 red pepper, roasted and
    skinned, cut into 8 strips
    (or use peppers from a jar)
Salt and freshly ground
    black pepper
Small handful flat-leaf
    parsley, chopped,
    to serve

For the griddled bread
4–8 thick slices bread
1 clove garlic, halved
2 tbsp olive oil

Heat the oil in a large frying pan or shallow casserole about 28cm in diameter over medium-low heat. Cook the onion and garlic until soft, 5 to 10 minutes. Add the ham and the *pimentón picante*, fry for 3 minutes, then add the chopped tomatoes and tomato paste. Cover the pan and cook until the tomatoes are reduced and pulpy, about 10 to 15 minutes.

Cook fresh peas for 3 minutes, then drain and refresh under cold water; frozen peas do not require precooking. Cook the green beans for 4 minutes, then drain and refresh under cold water.

Heat the oven to 200°C/gas 6, unless you choose to finish cooking on the hob.

Scatter the peas and beans over the tomato sauce in the pan. Break the eggs into the sauce. Arrange the chorizo slices around the eggs, and the red pepper strips over and around the eggs. Season with salt and pepper.

Bake until the egg whites are set and the yolks still soft, about 10 to 15 minutes, checking after 10. Alternatively, cook on the hob over a medium heat with a lid on the pan for 10 to 15 minutes. Meanwhile, rub the bread with the garlic, brush with the olive oil and griddle it on a ridged pan or in a frying pan. Scatter the chopped parsley over the dish and serve with griddled bread.

ROCKET SALAD WITH FIGS, PARMA HAM, GORGONZOLA & BASIL

═ SERVES SIX ═

I have two reasons for including this recipe. First, it's a celebration of all the great ingredients I found in Bologna's Mercato delle Erbe when I was there in the spring: lettuce and chicory in every shade from deep green to bright red, from pale green through pale pink to purple, plus prosciutto, Parma ham, Parmesan straight off the wheel and some fabulous Gorgonzola. And second because it's the sort of big salad you often find at lunch parties in Australia.

200g mixed bitter leaves:
cime di rapa, puntarelle,
radicchio, chicory,
curly endive
100g rocket leaves
6 ripe figs, quartered,
or 2 ripe white peaches,
stones removed, sliced
or 2 pears, peeled, cored
and sliced
10 slices Parma ham, torn
50g Parmesan cheese
shavings
90g Gorgonzola Dolce,
cut into chunks
500g ripe tomatoes, core
removed, cut into wedges
1 tbsp capers, drained
Handful basil leaves
40g toasted pine nuts
60ml olive oil
30ml sweet aged
balsamic vinegar

Mix the bitter leaves and rocket in a large serving bowl. Top with the figs or peaches or pears, ham, Parmesan, Gorgonzola, tomatoes, capers, basil leaves and pine nuts. Drizzle with olive oil and balsamic vinegar, toss well and serve.

INVOLTINI DI PESCE SPADA

≡ SERVES SIX ≡

I am very fond of swordfish involtini, a flattened fillet rolled round a stuffing of breadcrumbs, pine nuts, currants and pecorino, pinned with a cocktail stick, brushed with olive oil, rolled in breadcrumbs and baked. Wandering through the Ballarò street market in Palermo, you see giant trunks of swordfish that have been sliced on a bandsaw, pale and off-white, contrasting with similar-sized trunks of deep red tuna. This is a natural way of cooking this firm-fleshed fish. It's well worth buying a kilo or so to try it.

8 tbsp olive oil
1 onion, finely chopped
120g dried white
    Breadcrumbs (page 309)
40g currants
40g pine nuts, toasted
75g pecorino cheese, grated
Small handful flat-leaf
    parsley, leaves finely
    chopped
12 pitted green olives,
    chopped
8 turns black peppermill
6 swordfish slices, 1–1.5cm
    thick, skinned
18 cocktail sticks

For the fennel and
    orange salad
100g mixed leaves, such
    as frisée, endive, rocket
    or mustard leaves
1 large or 2 small bulbs
    fennel, finely sliced,
    reserving the fronds
3 oranges, peeled, pith
    removed and sliced
    into thin rounds
16 pitted green or black
    olives, halved
1½ tbsp orange juice
3 tbsp olive oil
½ tsp salt
8 turns black peppermill

Heat the oven to 190°C/gas 5.

Heat half the olive oil in a frying pan over medium heat, add the onion and gently sweat until soft, about 3 to 4 minutes. Add half the breadcrumbs and fry until golden, about 2 to 3 minutes. Remove from the heat and stir in the currants, pine nuts, pecorino, parsley, chopped green olives and black pepper.

Bash out the swordfish slices between 2 sheets of clingfilm with a meat mallet or rolling pin until about 4mm thick. Divide the stuffing mixture between the slices. Spread to within 1cm of the edges, then roll up the fish. Cut each roll into 3 pieces and secure with a cocktail stick. Brush with 2 tablespoons of the olive oil and roll in the remaining 60g breadcrumbs. Lightly oil a baking tray, arrange the fish rolls on it and drizzle with the remaining olive oil. Bake until the breadcrumbs are golden, 10 to 15 minutes.

Arrange the salad leaves on a platter or in a shallow bowl. Arrange the fennel, orange slices and olives on top. In a small glass, mix the orange juice, olive oil, salt and pepper with a fork, then drizzle over the salad. Decorate with the fennel fronds and serve at once with the fish.

RAVIOLI *WITH* PORCINI MUSHROOMS, SUN-DRIED TOMATOES & HAZELNUTS

=== SERVES EIGHT TO TEN ===

This recipe comes from Scacco Matto ('Checkmate') in Bologna. I was very taken with Chef Mario Ferrara's way of making and rolling pasta and the subtlety of the sweet onion stuffing. Everything about his cooking was a joy to watch. What I also liked was that the finished dish was not smothered in flavour, but rather that every element of it stood out. *Recipe photograph overleaf*

For the pasta
800g 00 pasta flour,
    plus extra for dusting
Few rasps nutmeg
1 tsp salt
8 eggs, beaten

For the filling
3 tbsp olive oil
300g onions, sliced
450ml water
¼ tsp fennel seeds, crushed
½ tsp salt
75g butter
75g plain flour
150g Parmesan cheese, grated
2 egg yolks
2g leaf gelatine, soaked for
    5 minutes in cold water

For the sauce
60g butter
4 tbsp olive oil
200g fresh porcini
    mushrooms, cut
    into large chunks
10 sun-dried tomatoes,
    finely sliced
Handful flat-leaf parsley,
    leaves chopped
75g hazelnuts, coarsely
    chopped, to serve

Make the pasta by combining the flour, nutmeg, salt and eggs in a food processor to 'breadcrumb' stage, then tip out on to a lightly floured board and knead for 3 to 4 minutes until smooth and elastic. Form into a ball, wrap in clingfilm and allow to rest for at least 30 minutes before rolling.

For the filling, warm the olive oil in a frying pan over medium heat and simmer the sliced onions for about 30 minutes until golden brown. Add the water, fennel seeds and salt, and simmer for 30 minutes to reduce by two-thirds. Transfer to a food processor and purée.

In a saucepan over medium heat, melt the butter, add the flour and stir for 1 to 2 minutes to make a roux. Add the onion purée, incorporate using a whisk, then cook for 2 minutes to thicken. Remove from the heat and add the Parmesan and egg yolks along with the gelatine leaf which you have squeezed of excess water. Stir until well incorporated, allow to cool then chill in the fridge.

Roll the pasta into sheets about 2mm thick and 8–10cm wide. Dot teaspoons of the onion mixture along the length of the pasta sheet to one side with a border of 5mm. Fold the opposite side over and press down around the filling. Cut into ravioli about 4cm square. Crimp the edges with your fingers to seal and set aside on a tray, keeping them separate. When ready, cook in boiling salted water for 3 to 4 minutes. Drain; reserving a little of the cooking water.

For the sauce, melt 30g of the butter with the olive oil in a frying pan over medium heat. Fry the porcini chunks for 2 to 3 minutes until softened, then add the sun-dried tomatoes, parsley and a tablespoon or two of pasta boiling water to loosen the sauce. Add the last knob of butter (30g) and the cooked ravioli to warm through. Serve topped with the chopped hazelnuts.

AÇORDA DE CAMARÃO
PORTUGUESE BREAD STEW *WITH* PRAWNS
SERVES FOUR TO SIX

I think what we love about a lot of the cooking of southern Europe is that it is frugal food. Think of dishes such as Fava Santorini (page 150), Caldo Verde (page 277) and the chickpea fritters in bread from Sicily called Panelle (page 151). They are all really good because they stem from human inventiveness in the face of limited resources. Prawn açorda – a bread stew with prawns – is another such dish. Made using good country bread, well-flavoured olive oil, lots of garlic and coriander and, above all, a deeply rich stock from prawn heads and shells, you get a creamy dish almost like a risotto in its consistency. Açorda is finished with beaten eggs, stirred in at the last minute to give it richness.

900g large raw
    shell-on prawns
1.2 litres water
4 tbsp olive oil
6 cloves garlic, peeled
1 red chilli, finely chopped
600g country-style crusty
    bread, such as sourdough,
    cut into chunks
1 tsp salt
8 turns black peppermill
4 eggs, beaten
Large handful
    coriander, chopped
1 lemon, cut into wedges,
    to serve

For the prawn stock
2 tbsp olive oil
Shells of the cooked prawns
1 small onion, chopped
3 cloves garlic,
    roughly chopped
1 tomato, quartered
½ tbsp tomato paste
200ml white wine
5 black peppercorns

Poach the prawns in the water for 3 to 4 minutes, depending on size, then drain and reserve the liquid. Peel the prawns, set aside and reserve the shells.

Make the stock in a separate pan over medium heat. Warm the olive oil and add the prawn shells. Fry for 5 to 10 minutes, bashing them with a wooden spoon to extract as much flavour as possible. Add the onion, garlic, tomato, tomato paste and white wine, bring to the boil and reduce the wine by half, then add the peppercorns and the liquor from cooking the prawns. Simmer the prawn stock for 30 minutes, strain through a fine sieve and discard the shells and vegetables. Measure 800ml of the stock, and set the rest aside for freezing.

Heat the olive oil for the açorda in a pan over a medium-low heat. Crush the cloves of garlic under the flat of a knife blade, add to the oil with the chilli and sweat the gently for 2 to 3 minutes. Add the stale bread chunks, the salt and the prawn stock, and cook until you have a thick bready mash. Taste for seasoning and add pepper. Add the prawns and heat through.

Take off the heat and stir in the beaten eggs; they will cook in the heat of the bread mash. Stir in most of the chopped coriander, reserving a little for garnish. Transfer to a warmed serving bowl and decorate with the reserved coriander. Serve immediately with lemon wedges.

METEOR SHOWER

≡ SERVES TWO ≡

Schønnemann is the oldest *smørrebrød* restaurant in Copenhagen. Walking into it is like stepping into a Hans Christian Andersen fairy story: low ceilings and faded, painted wooden dressers, Royal Copenhagen china and ship's lanterns over the tables, and a clientele to match. Half of them undoubtedly will have parked their bicycles outside. This dish is far and away the most ostentatious of the *smørrebrød* they do and the name reflects that. It's their most popular and it's delicious. I have simplified it because what is relatively easy to do in a restaurant is a bit pointless at home, but I hope I have got the essential scrumptiousness of the dish. *Recipe photograph overleaf*

4 skinned plaice fillets
Salt and freshly ground
    black pepper
2 tbsp flour
1 small egg, beaten
60g dried white *Breadcrumbs*
    (page 309) or Panko
    breadcrumbs
750ml sunflower or
    rapeseed oil, for frying
2 slices Danish rye bread,
    buttered
3 green asparagus spears,
    trimmed
Small handful mixed fresh
    parsley, dill and chives,
    finely chopped
3 tbsp *Mustard mayonnaise*
    (see page 308)
8–10 cooked North Atlantic
    prawns, peeled
1 tbsp Danish black caviar
Few sprigs dill, to dress
½ lemon, cut into wedges,
    to serve

Season the fillets on both sides. Set up 3 plates, 1 with flour, 1 with beaten egg and 1 with breadcrumbs. Coat each fillet on both sides first in flour, then egg, then breadcrumbs. Set aside while you heat the oil in a deep pan to 180°C, using a probe or sugar thermometer to check. Fry the plaice in batches until light golden, about 2 minutes on each side.

Arrange the fish on the buttered rye bread slices.

Boil the asparagus in salted water for 3 to 5 minutes (depending on size). Refresh under cold running water and cut in half lengthways.

Stir the herbs into the mayonnaise. Spoon the mayonnaise on top of the plaice, then arrange the prawns on top of the mayonnaise. Spoon the caviar on top and finish with the asparagus spears and a sprig of dill. Serve a lemon wedge alongside.

ARANCINI SALSICCIA

Until I went to Palermo recently I thought arancini were the size of ping-pong balls. In fact, they are the size of a tennis ball, perfect for lunch. It's a bit like picking up a Cornish pasty, and like pasties you don't need to sit down to eat them, but you can munch them while walking along. I am particularly fond of the sausagemeat filling for this one, with white wine, fennel and rosemary.

For the risotto
1.2–1.4 litres *Chicken stock*
   (page 307)
40g butter
300g Arborio or carnaroli
   risotto rice
Pinch saffron threads
50g Parmesan cheese,
   freshly grated
1 egg yolk

For the salsiccia filling
1 tbsp olive oil
225g coarse pork
   sausagemeat
1 small onion, finely chopped
1 small stick celery,
   finely chopped
1 clove garlic, finely
   chopped or grated
¾ tsp fennel seeds
Pinch chilli flakes
1 small sprig rosemary, leaves
   stripped and chopped
150ml dry white wine
½ tsp salt
6 turns black peppermill

To deep-fry
1 large egg, beaten
75g dried white *Breadcrumbs*
   (page 309)
1–1.5 litres vegetable oil

Heat the stock for the risotto in a saucepan. Melt the butter in a wide pan over medium-low heat, add the rice and stir well. Add a ladle of hot chicken stock along with the saffron and stir until absorbed, then continue to add the stock a ladleful at a time, stirring until it is all absorbed, about 20 minutes. Add the grated Parmesan and the egg yolk and stir. Spread on a baking tray, allow to cool, then transfer to the fridge and chill for 2 hours.

Prepare the filling. Warm the olive oil in a frying pan over a high heat and fry the sausagemeat, stirring often, until it is brown all over, about 5 to 10 minutes. Reduce the heat to medium, add the onion, celery and garlic and continue to fry until starting to soften, about 5 minutes. Add the fennel seeds, chilli flakes and rosemary and stir, then pour in the white wine. Reduce the white wine until it has almost disappeared. Remove from the heat and allow to cool to room temperature, then refrigerate until required.

When ready to fry, set up 2 bowls, 1 with the beaten egg, 1 with the dried breadcrumbs. With damp hands, take a sixth of the risotto on your palm. Using the back of a spoon, spread and press the rice to cover your palm and closed fingers. Add a heaped tablespoon of the sausage filling on the middle and mould the rice around it to form a tennis-ball-sized arancino. Set aside. Repeat until all 6 are made.

Heat the oven to 130°C/gas 1.

Heat the oil in a deep pan to 160°C. Use a sugar thermometer or probe to check. Put a plate lined with kitchen paper next to the pan. Roll each ball in beaten egg then breadcrumbs and lower 2 at a time into the oil using a slotted spoon. Cook for 8 to 10 minutes until golden brown all over. Transfer to the lined plate to absorb excess oil. Keep warm in the oven while you fry the remainder. Serve warm or cool.

BREADS, PASTRIES & AFTERNOON CAKES

In 1978 I took a kitchen timer into my City & Guilds pastry exam at Camborne College. The examiner who presided over us sixteen Advanced Pastry students said he wasn't happy about it, but could find nothing in the rules to prohibit it. It seemed to me to be the obvious thing to do for accuracy in pastry. In the exam we had to make a millefeuille filled with pastry cream, hand-making the puff pastry and finishing the top with white icing decorated with black criss-crosses created with red-hot skewers. Then came a charlotte russe with a filling of a bavarois. We also had to make a simple genoise, spin some sugar over a broom handle and create a bombe Alaska. I've never considered myself to be much of a pastry cook but passing this exam made me much more confident. Fast forward and five years later I found myself in the Seafood Restaurant kitchen; the sous chef had left because his wife had died and under the subsequent strain two other chefs had gone, falling like dominoes. The complaint about the sweets on offer that night was so vehement that I finally sent a message out to the customers explaining that, out of necessity, I had taken over the desserts myself that evening. So I know I am not the neatest pastry cook, but I can do it if needed and I do enjoy it.

One of the great pleasures of going to so many interesting cities for *Long Weekends* has been visiting some of the best cities in the world for pastries, breads and cakes – just the sort of things you might want to cook over the weekend. You will probably be familiar with the Portuguese custard tarts called *pastéis de nata*. My recipe (page 107) calls for you to make your own puff pastry: it's time-consuming but unforgettable. The *canelés* from Bordeaux (page 104) have an unbelievably crisp, caramel-scented finish. You might like to try your hand at a Sachertorte, too (page 114), or maybe over a couple of days the Danish-style Sourdough on page 120. I'm rather proud of this. My friend Paul Cunningham, who has lived and worked in Denmark for years, gave me a jar of sourdough starter in Copenhagen, saying, 'This is Helena Christensen.'

'What?'

'Don't you know that all sourdough starters have women's names, like fishing boats?'

I must say, it makes a very pretty sourdough bread. It is, hopefully, soon to appear on the shelves of our own patisserie.

CANELÉ

The first thing I should say about canelé, apart from the fact that it is the most wonderful accompaniment to a café noir, is not to bother with the silicone moulds you find on the internet. You have to buy the metal ones, and if you coat them with beeswax before baking you will be rewarded with the most deliciously crisp caramelized surface to the pastry. It's the combination of the crust and the soft, almost custardy interior flavoured with rum that makes it so special.

500ml full-fat milk
50g unsalted butter
5 large egg yolks,
   lightly beaten
120g plain flour, sifted
250g icing sugar, sifted
½ tsp fine table salt, sifted
4 tsp vanilla extract
75ml dark/gold rum

To line the moulds
30g unsalted butter
30g food-grade beeswax,
   chopped or coarsely grated

In a pan, heat the milk with the butter until the butter has melted, then take it off the heat and let it cool until tepid. Stir in the egg yolks, then the dry ingredients. Combine well without incorporating air, then pass through a sieve into a clean bowl and stir in the vanilla extract and rum. Cover with clingfilm and leave to rest for 24 to 48 hours in the fridge, stirring once.

A couple of hours before you plan to cook the canelé, combine the butter and beeswax in a small pan over a low heat, or in a bain-marie, and melt until combined. Briefly warm the 12 metal moulds, then brush with the mixture. Turn them upside down on a sheet of greaseproof paper to stop the butter and beeswax pooling in the crevices. Transfer to a freezer and chill for an hour.

Canelé are best eaten 1 to 4 hours after baking. When ready to bake, heat the oven to 250°C/gas 9. Pour the cold batter into the cold moulds to about 1cm from the top. Bake for 15 minutes. Turn the heat down to 190°C/gas 5 and cook for a further 30 minutes. The canelé should not soufflé up beyond the top of the mould, so don't be expecting that. At this point turn one out and check for colour: it should be a deep dark brown and feel crispy on the outside with a little give when squeezed. If not brown and crispy enough, return to the tin. When done, turn out and allow to cool on a wire rack. Resist eating for an hour.

BERLINER DOUGHNUTS

≡ MAKES TEN ≡

Doughnuts are everywhere in Berlin, specifically the round ones, not the ring ones. The filling is most often plum jam. The joke is that in Germany they are described as Berliners but in Berlin itself they are not; they are called *Pfannkuchen*.

250g white bread flour, sifted
250g plain white flour, sifted, plus extra for dusting
½ tsp salt
7g sachet fast-acting yeast
200ml full-fat milk
3 tbsp golden caster sugar
50g butter, cubed
2 large eggs, beaten
1 tsp vanilla extract
Zest 1 lemon
1–1.5 litres rapeseed oil, for frying
100g icing or golden caster sugar, for coating
340g jar jam, plum, cherry or blackcurrant

In the large bowl of a food mixer, mix the two flours with the salt. Sprinkle the yeast on top.

In a saucepan, warm the milk with the caster sugar and butter. As soon as the butter melts, take the milk off the heat. You don't want it too hot or it will kill the yeast.

Stir the eggs, vanilla extract and lemon zest into the milk, then add the liquid to the flour and yeast. Using a dough hook, bring the mixture together and knead for 5 to 10 minutes. Lightly oil a fresh bowl and transfer the dough to this. Cover with clingfilm and allow to rise until doubled in bulk.

When risen, turn out on to a lightly floured board and roll out to a sheet about 2.5cm thick. Using a pastry cutter about 8cm in diameter, cut out circles of dough. Roll the leftovers and repeat until used up. Put the circles of dough on a lightly oiled baking sheet, cover with a clean tea towel and allow to rise for about 45 to 60 minutes.

Heat the oil in a large, deep pan to 175°C, using a probe or sugar thermometer to check. Line a plate with several sheets of kitchen paper and place alongside. Using a long-handled spoon, carefully lower the dough into the oil a few at a time (so as not to cool down the oil too much). Fry each side for about 2 minutes, by which time they should be puffed up and golden. Remove from the oil with a slotted spoon and transfer to the lined plate. Tip the icing or caster sugar on to a separate plate and roll the doughnuts into the sugar while they are still hot. Allow to cool a little then, using the handle of a wooden spoon, make a hole in the side. With a piping bag, pipe jam into the hole until it feels full. Serve while still warm or at most within a couple of hours of frying.

PORTUGUESE CUSTARD TARTS

MAKES ABOUT TWENTY-EIGHT

I have been told the Portuguese pastries at the Co-op supermarket in the UK are rather good. However, that was after I had spent quite some time making these, in memory of the total delight I found everywhere in Lisbon. So I got the person who gave me the recommendation to bring a couple down to Padstow and, yes, they were good, but nothing to compare with my tarts straight out of the oven, with their crisp pastry and lovely silky custard. Best eaten in the morning on the streets of Lisbon or in your kitchen just after baking.

For the pastry
300g plain flour, sifted,
    plus extra for dusting
¼ tsp salt
200ml water
225g unsalted butter, softened

For the filling
40g plain flour
310ml full-fat milk
250g granulated sugar
150ml water
6cm cinnamon stick
1 tsp vanilla extract
6 large egg yolks, beaten
1 tsp icing sugar mixed with
    1 tsp ground cinnamon,
    to serve, plus extra icing
    sugar for browning,
    if needed

Put the flour, salt and water in a food mixer fitted with a dough hook, and combine until you have a soft, bread-like dough, about 5 minutes. It should leave the sides of the bowl clean.

On a well-floured work surface, form the dough into an 18cm square, then roll it out into a 45cm square. Brush any excess flour off the top and trim any wavy edges. Spread two-thirds of the square with a third of the soft butter, stopping shy of the edges. Fold the unbuttered third over the middle third and fold the remaining third over that.

Flour the board again and rotate the pastry 90 degrees. Roll out again to a 45cm square and repeat the buttering, using a further third of the butter and the same folding process.

Flour the board again, rotate the pastry by 90 degrees again, and roll into a rectangle 35cm x 45cm, with the shorter edge nearest you. Spread with the remaining butter and fold one last time, as before.

For the rolling, turn the folded pastry 90 degrees and roll out the dough to a rectangle 45cm x 55cm, with the shorter side nearest you. Neatly and tightly roll the pastry away from you into a long sausage, so that in cross-section you have a spiral roll of dough. Wrap the roll in clingfilm and chill for at least 2 hours.

For the filling, mix the flour and 4 tablespoons of the milk in a bowl until smooth.

Recipe continued overleaf

Recipe continued

Put the sugar, water and cinnamon stick in a saucepan and bring to a rolling boil.

In a separate saucepan, scald the rest of the milk – bring it almost to the boil then immediately take it off the heat. Whisk the hot milk into the flour paste. Remove the cinnamon stick before pouring the sugar syrup into the hot milk-and-flour mixture, stirring all the time. Add the vanilla and allow to cool slightly before whisking in the beaten egg yolks. Strain the custard into a clean jug, cover the surface with clingfilm, and set aside.

Heat the oven to 250°C/gas 9, or as hot as it will go.

Remove the pastry roll from the fridge. Roll until it is about 2½cm in diameter, then cut it into 28 even slices. Put a slice of pastry in each hole of 2 or 3 patty tins (no need to butter the tin as the pastry is buttery enough). Dip your fingers and thumbs into a bowl of cold water and press down to flatten the base and to mould the pastry up the sides so it stands just proud of the lip.

Fill each pastry cup with the custard. Bake until the edges of pastries are deep golden brown and the custards are browned, about 9 to 11 minutes. If the oven is not hot enough to get a good colour on the tartlets, then dust with icing sugar and use a blow torch, if you have one, or a blast under a hot grill, to get the characteristic brown spots on the surface.

Remove from the oven and to cool a few minutes in the tins before transferring to a wire rack. Eat warm or at room temperature, dusted with icing sugar and cinnamon.

FRITTELLE DI RISO
ENRICA'S RICE PUDDING FRITTERS
═ MAKES EIGHT TO TEN ═

Enrica Lazzarini has a blog called bolognafood.it. It's a good idea to catch up with a few local bloggers in a city because they tend to be enthusiastic and patriotic about their city's cooking. Not only were Enrica's rice cakes fabulous, she also took us to the sort of bar you never forget. It reminded me of The Dolphin opposite the old fish market in Plymouth during the years when the market was still open there and the pub was filled with an extraordinary range of people: fishermen, of course, market traders and box shifters, students, hippies, fans of the pub, like me, Keith Floyd and David Pritchard, and the usual collection of drunks very keen to have a long conversation with you. The Osteria del Sole bar likewise was slightly dodgy but being close to the university also had undergraduates and professors, as well as a few tables with families eating their own food – because the pub doesn't cook anything, you are allowed to bring whatever you make and, it being Italy, indeed they do. Enrica produced these rice cakes, plus some slices of local mortadella called *salame rosa* and a basket of freshly baked, puffed-up *crescentine fritte* to make sandwiches of the meat. There was also a local comfit called *mostarda bolognese* and a most wonderful yeast cake filled with chocolate cream. But the star turn were the *frittelle di riso,* well worth making I say. Chief fascination for me, as well as all the delicious food, was a party of slightly overweight and overdressed local women who could have come straight from a Beryl Cook painting.

100g pudding rice
500ml full-fat milk
Zest 1 lemon
1 vanilla pod, split,
    or 1 tsp vanilla extract
100g caster sugar
1 egg, beaten
70g plain flour
Pinch salt
100g raisins, soaked for
    15 minutes in cognac
    liqueur or boiling water
500ml vegetable oil,
    for deep-frying
About 50g granulated
    sugar, for dredging

Cook the rice in the milk with the lemon zest and split vanilla pod, or vanilla extract, bring up to a scald then reduce the heat and cook gently until the rice is tender; this should take about 15 to 20 minutes.

Remove from the heat and let the mixture get cool. Remove the lemon zest and the vanilla pod, and incorporate the sugar and egg, mixing well, then the flour, salt and the drained sultanas. Mix well and allow to rest for 2 hours in the fridge.

In a medium-sized pan, heat the oil to 180°C, using a probe or sugar thermometer to test. Fry dessertspoons of the mixture until a deep golden brown on both sides. Drain on paper towels, dredge in sugar and serve.

GERMAN APPLE CAKE

⸺ SERVES EIGHT ⸺

This dish comes from Zur Letzten Instanz, one of the oldest restaurants in Berlin, built right by the wall of the medieval city. If you are visiting Berlin it's something of a must. It is dark and many-roomed and you need to prepare for a massive intake of food. Not only is the *Eisbein* – fat-covered pork knuckle – the biggest I have ever seen, but even if you order something like liver you get a mountain of mashed potato alongside, and the Königsberger Klopse (see page 204) were like cricket balls. I loved it all, though how you could finish that pork knuckle I still don't understand. But what I really loved was the apple cake afterwards. The Germans and Austrians, rather than dusting with icing sugar, sprinkle their cakes with demerara before cooking, which gives the cakes a lovely crunch. *Recipe photograph overleaf*

2 dessert apples, peeled,
   cored and cut into
   fine wedges
1 tbsp lemon juice
125g unsalted butter,
   softened
140g golden caster sugar
3 eggs, beaten
225g plain flour
2 tsp baking powder
½ tsp salt
75ml full-fat milk

For the topping
1½ tbsp demerara sugar
½ tsp ground cinnamon
Whipped cream, to serve

Heat the oven to 170°C/gas 3. Butter and line a 23cm diameter cake tin.

Coat the apples in the lemon juice and set aside. In a large bowl, beat together the butter and sugar until pale and fluffy using an electric beater. Add eggs and beat until smooth. Sift in the flour, baking powder and salt. Mix until well incorporated. Slowly add the milk, mixing well after each addition until you have a smooth batter.

Transfer the batter to the cake tin. Arrange the apple wedges in a spiral over the batter. Mix the sugar and cinnamon together and sprinkle on top. Bake in the middle of the oven for 40 to 45 minutes, until a skewer inserted in the centre of the cake comes out clean and the top is golden.

Remove the cake from the oven and cool for 15 minutes in the tin. Run a knife around the edges and turn out on to a wire rack. Serve warm or at room temperature with whipped cream.

SACHERTORTE À LA SACHER

═ SERVES EIGHT TO TWELVE ═

I ate Sachertorte all my life until my aunt Zoe died. Though very German/Austrian in her habits, she professed to disliking both countries, but this was because of her difficult time as a child in England during the First World War. Her house had that spare, clean and tidy look of most Germanic interiors, and she made the best Sachertorte. Hers had three layers of apricot jam as she cut her cake into three tiers. The original Sachertorte from Demel in Vienna has one layer of jam, and the official Sacher-Torte from the Sacher Hotel has two layers, so Aunt Zoe was going the extra distance, and the result was a lovely, fruity, chocolate cake.

140g butter at room
    temperature, plus
    extra for greasing
110g icing sugar
Seeds ½ vanilla pod
6 eggs, separated
140g plain flour, plus
    extra for dusting
130g dark chocolate
110g caster sugar
300g apricot jam,
    warmed and sieved
Whipped cream, to serve

For the chocolate sugar glaze
400g caster sugar
200g dark chocolate
    (70 per cent cocoa
    solids), chopped
250ml water

Heat the oven to 180°C/gas 4. Line the bottom of a 23cm springform cake tin with baking parchment and grease the sides with butter. Sprinkle in a little flour, then shake out excess.

In a bowl, whisk the butter with the icing sugar and vanilla seeds until pale and creamy. Gradually add the egg yolks and continue beating until well combined, then add the plain flour.

Melt the chocolate in a bowl set over a pan of simmering water, then fold into the egg mixture.

Whisk the egg whites until stiff, then sprinkle in the sugar and continue to beat until stiff and glossy. Loosen the cake mix with a big spoon of 'meringuey' egg whites. Fold in the rest with a large metal spoon, until incorporated.

Pour in the prepared tin and spread the surface evenly with a spatula. Bake for 55 to 60 minutes. The cake should be firm but springy, and a skewer should come out clean. Cool in the tin for 20 minutes, then release the spring, peel off the baking paper and continue to cool.

When entirely cool, use a bread knife to cut the cake horizontally into thirds. Spread each layer with apricot jam. Reassemble the cake, using the bottom for the top. Set it on a wire rack over a tray (to collect drips) and allow to dry a little while you make the glaze.

Put the sugar, chocolate and water in a medium saucepan over medium heat to dissolve the sugar and melt the chocolate. Bring up to the boil and keep boiling until a temperature of 112°C is reached; use a sugar thermometer or temperature probe to check.

Pour the hot glaze immediately over the cake and allow it to run down the sides, spreading the mixture until the cake is covered and glossy. Leave to cool and harden a little before serving.

TRIGONA PANORAMATOS
BAKED FILO PASTRIES
WITH VANILLA CREAM

MAKES TWENTY-FOUR

Pastries are one of the glories of Thessaloniki cuisine. The city is stuffed full of pastry shops, all specializing in their own particular one. Elenidis is famous for creating and selling the *trigona*, a filo pastry triangle filled with custard.

12 sheets filo pastry
125g unsalted butter, melted

For the syrup
350g granulated sugar
250ml water
1 cinnamon stick

For the crème patissière
500ml full-fat milk
4 large egg yolks
100g caster sugar
40g plain flour
40g cornflour
100ml double cream
2 tsp vanilla extract
30g shelled pistachios,
    coarsely chopped

Heat the oven to 180°C/gas 4.

Make the filo triangles. Take one sheet of filo at a time on to a board; cover the rest with a clean, slightly damp tea towel. Cut the filo lengthways into 2 long strips and brush with a little melted butter. Fold each strip lengthways in half and brush with a little more butter. Take the bottom corner and fold it up to its opposite edge to form an angle. Fold this upwards along a horizontal fold. Make another angle fold, this time going to the other side. Keep doing this for the whole length of the strip. Brush with butter and place on a baking sheet. Continue with the remaining filo pastry until you have 24 triangles. Bake for 12 to 15 minutes until a deep golden brown. Allow to cool on a wire rack, before slipping a sharp-tipped knife into one side of the triangle to open them up a little.

For the syrup, put the sugar, water and cinnamon in a saucepan. Dissolve the sugar over a low heat, then turn up the heat and bring to the boil. Simmer for 10 minutes until thick; it shouldn't need stirring.

Place a wire rack over a tray. Using tongs, dip the filo triangles in the syrup for about 10 seconds on each side, allow excess to drip back, then place on the wire rack and leave to dry.

Scald the milk in a pan. In a bowl, mix the egg yolks, caster sugar and both flours to a stiff paste; if too stiff, loosen with a splash of cold milk. Whisk in the scalded milk. Return to the rinsed pan and whisk over medium heat until thick. It might go through a lumpy stage, but keep whisking and it will come together again. Allow to cool.

Whisk in the cream and vanilla extract. Transfer to a piping bag fitted with a large plain nozzle. Pipe into the open end of the filo triangles. Sprinkle over the pistachios and serve immediately.

GENOVESI ERICINE
SICILIAN LEMON TARTS
MAKES EIGHT

I have to confess I got this recipe from the internet, meaning to go to Palermo and try the real thing. But when I got there, I couldn't find them. Every time I said *ericine* they pointed to *arancini*. I know, not so similar, but then perhaps you haven't heard me try to speak Italian. Anyway, the *arancini salsiccia* on page 96, almost the size of cricket balls, are excellent, and in the end I did find *ericine* and modified the internet recipe. It's exquisitely lemony and creamy. Traditionally they are served while still slightly warm with strong coffee.

For the pastry
125g semolina
125g plain flour, plus
   extra for dusting
100g caster sugar
100g butter, at room
   temperature, diced
2 egg yolks
2 tbsp very cold water
1 tbsp icing sugar,
   for dusting

For the filling
1 egg yolk
70g caster sugar
30g cornflour
200ml milk
Zest and juice
   1 large lemon

Mix the semolina with the flour, sugar, butter and egg yolks in a food processor and pulse until the mixture looks crumbly. Add the water and pulse to bring together. Turn out in a lightly floured surface and knead for 1 to 2 minutes until the dough forms a smooth ball. Wrap in clingfilm and chill for about 30 minutes.

Make the filling. Mix the egg yolk and sugar in a bowl with an electric whisk. Slake the cornflour with a little of the milk and then incorporate it into the remaining milk. Stir well and gradually add the milk to the beaten egg yolk, whisking all the time. Transfer to a pan and heat gently, stirring continuously for 3 to 4 minutes until it is really thick. Stir in the lemon juice and zest and cover the surface with clingfilm to prevent a skin forming. Set aside to cool.

Heat the oven to 220°C/gas 7.

Roll the dough on a lightly floured board into a sheet about 4mm thick. Cut 16 discs using an 8cm or 9cm pastry cutter.

Put 1½ to 2 tablespoons of the lemon filling in the centre of 8 of the discs. Cover them with the remaining discs. Pinch the edges with your fingers to seal well.

Bake for 7 minutes, or until golden. Watch them carefully as the sugar in the pastry means it burns easily. Cool slightly on a wire rack, then sprinkle with icing sugar and serve.

DANISH-STYLE SOURDOUGH RYE BREAD

=== MAKES ONE LARGE LOAF ===

I got this recipe from John Sterchi at the Mirabelle bakery in Copenhagen. The Mirabelle is a wonderful place to buy the best possible sourdough and to sit and drink espresso coffee as good as you can get in Australia or New Zealand, as well as, not surprisingly, the world's best Danish – though in fact Danish pastries originally came from Vienna. A chef friend of mine, Paul Cunningham, gave me the sourdough starter for this bread. If you can get starter from a friend, so much the better. If not, see page 309 for how to make your own.

24 hours before baking
130g rye flour
60ml *Sourdough starter*
  (page 309)
300ml warm water
50g flax seeds
50g sunflower seeds
75ml water

On baking day
500ml starter (the mixture
  from the day before)
250g rye flour
100g cracked rye grains
  (or 350g rye flour total
  if unavailable)
1 tsp salt
1½ tbsp treacle
1½ tbsp rice malt
  extract/malt extract
50–125ml water (quantity
  depends on how wet
  the starter is)
Vegetable oil, for greasing
1 tsp sunflower seeds
  (optional)
1 tbsp jumbo oats (optional)

Twenty-four hours before baking, mix the flour, starter and warm water in a bowl. Cover with clingfilm and set aside at room temperature for 24 hours. Soak the seeds in the water in a bowl and set alongside the starter mixture for 24 hours.

On baking day, mix the starter from yesterday, along with the soaked seeds and any soaking liquid, with the rye flour, rye grains, salt, treacle, rice malt extract and water. Mix well. You should have a stiff dough, like a fairly thick cake batter. If it looks too dry, add a little more water. It is not like a traditional wheat bread dough and is not kneaded.

Grease a loaf tin about 23cm x 13cm and 8cm deep really well with vegetable oil and, if you like, scatter some sunflower seeds in the base. Spoon the dough into the tin, smooth the top and, again if you like, scatter the surface with oats. Leave it to rise in a warmish place for anything from 4 to 8 hours (depending on temperature) until it has doubled in bulk.

Heat the oven to 190°C/gas 5 and bake for 80 to 90 minutes. Check after an hour. If it is browning too much, cover with a sheet of foil. The bread should shrink a little from the sides and leave the tin easily when ready. Cool on a wire rack.

This bread is best left for 24 hours before cutting and eating. It will last for a week without freezing.

KNÆKBROED
DANISH CRACKER BREAD
SERVES FOUR TO SIX

This is possibly the best crisp rye bread you are ever going to taste, and it's simple to make. A delicious alternative to a cracker; great with smoked fish, pâté, cheese or cooked meats.

50g medium oatmeal
50g sesame seeds
50g flax seeds
50g sunflower seeds
100g spelt flour
75g rye flour
½ tsp baking powder
½ tsp salt
50ml sunflower/rapeseed oil
100ml water
Sea salt flakes and/or extra
    seeds to sprinkle on top

Heat the oven to 180°C/gas 4.

Mix all the ingredients together into a dough. Place between 2 sheets of baking parchment and roll out to about 3mm thick. Discard the top layer of parchment. Turn the dough out on to a large baking sheet and discard the other layer of parchment. Either cut into cracker-shaped rectangles, or leave whole to break once baked into pieces of irregular size and shape.

Sprinkle with a few extra seeds and flakes of sea salt, if desired. Bake until dried out and crisp, with a little colour: 20 to 25 minutes.

SATURDAY NIGHT NIBBLES & STARTERS

ICELANDIC ROLLMOPS, SMOKED TROUT PATE & SMOKED MACKEREL WIH PICKLED RHUBARB 128

BEETROOT-CURED SALMON WITH CUCUMBER & APPLE PICKLE 134

ROAST BEEF ECLAIRS WITH RED ONION MARMALADE & HORSERADISH CREAM 137

SHALLOTS STUFFED WITH LAMB, CINNAMON & PINE NUTS 139

BAKED FETA CHEESE WITH TOMATO, RED PEPPER & CHILLIS 142

SALT COD FRITTERS 144

PRAWN FRIED DUMPLINGS 145

SLICED BELLY PORK WITH SMOKED PAPRIKA & CUMIN SEEDS 148

PUREÉ OF SPLIT YELLOW PEAS WITH GARLIC, THYME, RED ONION & CAPERS 150

CHICKPEA & FENNEL SEED FRITTERS 151

CHILLED TOMATO SOUP WITH SERRANO HAM & TUNA FLAKES 154

SICILIAN PIZZA 155

HALIBUT SOUP WITH CREAM, APPLE & DILL 158

SASHIMI 162

OCTOPUS SALAD WITH RED ONION, GARLIC & PARSLEY 163

SOUP OF HAKE WITH SEVILLE, ORANGES & SAFFRON 166

MONKFISH FRITTERS WITH CUMIN, GARLIC & PIMENTON 168

TORTELLINI IN BRODO 171

SALAD OF CANNELINI BEANS, RED ONIONS, PEPPERS & TOMATOES 174

SALAD OF GRILLED TOMATOES WITH ROCKET & BALSAMIC VINEGAR 175

'Saturday night's alright for fighting'
ELTON JOHN & BERNIE TAUPIN

Not so much the fighting, but Saturday is a night to let rip, and that's what I love about the song. When I was cooking every day at the Seafood Restaurant, Saturday night was the big one, almost like waiting on stage for the curtain to rise, adrenalin running. Even cooking at home on Saturday night feels like that. It's the time to push the boat out, but it has to be a controlled launch, which is where nibbles come in handy. If you're going to produce a show-stopping main course, I advise starting the evening with dishes already made for your guests to start nibbling at. In this way, should there be an unforeseen mishap and you are still, unbelievably, cooking when everyone arrives, they can be diverted to snacking rather than talking too much to you and increasing your already barely concealed panic. A very good friend of mine, Matt Preston, one of the presenters of *Australian Masterchef*, said in one of his books that if you're having people round for a big dinner, aim to have all the food ready and the cooking utensils washed up and put away at least half an hour before your guests arrive. In my case, I would say an hour, though miraculously that will dwindle to five minutes on the night.

The great pleasure of nibbles is that you can forget about a first course and go straight into the main afterwards. Things like slices of Beetroot-cured Salmon with Cucumber and Apple Pickle (page 134) or the stuffed shallots from Thessaloniki on page 139, or the octopus salad, Salada de Polvo, on page 163, or a dish that works very well for me, the chicharrones from Cadiz on page 148. Most of these, of course, will make very nice starters as well. You can also play it the other way around: very simple nibbles – such as salted nuts or sliced tomatoes with basil or salami – followed by a more elaborate first-course dish such as the Halibut Soup on page 158 or the Sashimi on page 162. In this category would be the Salt Cod Fritters or the similar prawn ones, Rissóis de Camarão, on pages 144 and 145, which, in a perfect world, require cooking at the last minute. A difficult undertaking, I know, for a large party, and if you decide to do it make sure you serve a main course that can be fully prepared in advance, such as the Viennese Gulasch on page 195.

ICELANDIC ROLLMOPS, SMOKED TROUT PÂTÉ & SMOKED MACKEREL WITH PICKLED RHUBARB

I have grouped these three recipes together because they make the perfect accompaniments to the hotspring rye bread. I am not suggesting you have to make all three at the same time, but I am always looking for nice recipes for nibbles and these all fit the bill. There is nothing to the smoked mackerel: just cut it into a neat piece and put on the rye bread. The herring rollmops take a little time but they do keep for a couple of weeks in the fridge. Serve them on bread with a little sour cream or skyr (Icelandic fat-free yoghurt), or use them in the Viennese recipe on page 299. The recipe for the pâté comes from Australia; it is completely delicious even though I say so myself. *Recipe photograph overleaf*

ICELANDIC HOTSPRING RYE BREAD

I've mentioned the joy of eating this rye bread straight out of the hot sand in Iceland in the main introduction on page 11. It's well worth making even without the advantage of a source of geothermal heat.

Butter, for greasing
600g rye flour
300g plain white flour
300g golden caster sugar
4 tsp baking powder
1 tsp fine salt
1 litre full-fat milk

Heat the oven to 100°C/gas ¼. Use butter to grease a casserole dish with a tight-fitting lid.

Mix the ingredients together into a fairly loose paste – it doesn't form a dough like regular bread. Put it in the casserole, cover with the lid and bake for about 7 hours. It should be well risen and cooked through. Transfer to a wire rack to cool.

Cut into squares and serve with smoked mackerel, smoked trout pâté (page 131) or rollmops.

ICELANDIC ROLLMOPS

SERVES FOUR WITH RYE BREAD AS A STARTER

8 herring fillets,
    pin-boned, skin left on
40g fine salt dissolved
    in 400ml water
100g caster sugar
500ml cider vinegar
1 tbsp pickling spice:
    mixed yellow mustard
    seeds, black peppercorns,
    white peppercorns,
    coriander seeds
Sprig thyme
4 allspice berries
Bay leaf
1 small onion, finely sliced

Put the herring fillets in the brine and leave for 2 to 3 hours.

In a pan, dissolve the sugar in the vinegar, add the pickling spices, thyme, allspice and bay leaf and bring up to a simmer. Cook for 1 to 2 minutes, then take off the heat and leave to cool and infuse.

Drain the herrings and discard the brine. Pat the fillets dry with kitchen paper and roll them up, skin-side outermost. Secure with a cocktail stick. Layer the herring rolls with the sliced onion in a sterilized 1-litre Kilner-type jar. Pour the vinegar mixture, spices and all, into the jar.

Seal the jar and store in the fridge for at least 3 days before eating. The herrings are best consumed within 10 days.

SMOKED TROUT PÂTÉ

125g smoked trout
50g butter
55g natural Greek yoghurt
2 tbsp olive oil
1 tsp lemon juice
½ tsp caster sugar
1 tsp chopped dill
5 turns black peppermill

Put all the ingredients into a food processor and pulse to a smooth pâté.

QUICK PICKLED RHUBARB

═ MAKES THREE 340G JARS ═

Delicious with any oily or smoked fish, especially mackerel. Buy smoked fillets and cut into neat 2.5cm squares to serve on top of squares of rye bread. The pickles will keep in the fridge for up to 1 month.

500ml cider vinegar
300g granulated sugar
1½ tbsp salt
½ tsp yellow mustard seeds
6 black peppercorns
3cm root ginger, peeled
   and thinly sliced
Zest 1 orange, pared
   with a potato peeler
450g fresh rhubarb,
   washed well and cut
   into 2cm lengths

In a medium saucepan, combine the vinegar, sugar, salt, mustard seeds and peppercorns. Cook over medium heat, stirring occasionally, until the sugar is just dissolved. Take off the heat, add the ginger and orange zest and allow the liquid to cool to room temperature.

Divide the rhubarb between 3 340g glass jars and ladle in the cooled pickling mixture. Top with the lids and refrigerate for 2 days before eating.

BEETROOT-CURED SALMON
WITH CUCUMBER & APPLE PICKLE

=== SERVES TEN ===

Like many other northern European cities, Berlin has many recipes for cured salmon. Smoked and salted fish is wonderful in many different countries, but I was particularly struck by the display in KaDeWe, a department store whose name I cannot see without remembering a song from the late and much-lamented David Bowie, 'Where Are We Now?' which is all about Berlin. At the counter were every type of herring, including bloaters and red herring, salt fish, smoked sprats, smoked cod's roe and about four or five different cured salmon dishes, one being a beetroot cure, of which I have come up with my own version, which marries the flavour of beetroot with caraway seeds and white pepper. The salad is an amalgam of similar accompaniments from restaurants all over Berlin, though the main inspiration came from a restaurant called La Soupe Populaire. The cured salmon keeps in the fridge for three to four days, and also freezes well.

For the cure
250g beetroot, boiled
    until tender, peeled
100g coarse sea salt
75g white sugar
2 tsp caraway seeds, crushed
    or coarsely ground
2 tsp white peppercorns,
    crushed
1kg salmon fillet in
    2 pieces of 500g each

For the salad
4 dessert apples,
    peeled and cored
1 small red onion, peeled
2 cucumbers
6 tsp cider vinegar
2 tsp rapeseed oil
2 tsp horseradish cream
½ tsp salt
1 tsp sugar
Small handful dill fronds,
    roughly chopped

Put the cooked beetroot, sea salt, sugar, caraway seeds and white pepper into a blender and blitz to a purée.

Smear the cure all over the salmon flesh and sandwich the fillets together with the skin-side outermost. Wrap in 2 or 3 layers of clingfilm and lift on to a shallow tray. Rest a smaller tray or chopping board on top and weigh it down with tins or weights. Refrigerate for 2 days, turning the fish every 12 hours.

When ready to serve, discard any excess cure from the salmon. Slice as you would smoked salmon: across the fillet in thin slices with the knife at an angle, then close to the skin to release the flesh. Arrange on a serving plate.

For the salad, using a mandolin or a very sharp knife, slice the apple, red onion and cucumber into wafer-thin slices and put in a bowl. Combine the cider vinegar, oil, horseradish cream, salt and sugar to make a dressing and pour over the salad. Toss well. Dress with the dill. Serve alongside the salmon.

ROAST BEEF ÉCLAIRS
WITH RED ONION MARMALADE
& HORSERADISH CREAM

MAKES ABOUT TWENTY-FIVE

Nowhere but Berlin could you go a function in an old crematorium. David, the director, and I had enormous fun discussing how *noir* Berlin is and it don't get much *noirer* than this. We had such an enjoyable evening with chef Markus Bongardt and maître d' Christian Wilke. I particularly liked this little canapé, which was the first of a many-course dinner. It's the sort of thing that would be a big hit at any drinks party. Once you have mastered the relatively simple task of cooking choux pastry, the rest is just assembly.

For the choux pastry
55g cold butter, cubed
150ml water
70g plain flour
Pinch fine salt
2 eggs, beaten

For the red onion marmalade
40g butter
250g red onions, finely sliced
2 tbsp demerara sugar
40ml balsamic vinegar
100ml red wine
1 tsp quince or
    redcurrant jelly
½ tsp salt
5 turns black peppermill

For the horseradish cream
1 tbsp freshly grated
    horseradish (or creamed
    if not available)
1 tsp fresh lemon juice
Zest ½ lemon
1 tsp Dijon mustard
150ml crème fraîche
Pinch salt

For the beef
250g sirloin or fillet steak
1 tsp olive oil, for brushing
Salt and freshly ground
    black pepper
Rocket or watercress
    leaves, to finish

Begin by making the red onion marmalade. In a large pan over a low heat, melt the butter then stir in the onions and sugar. Cook very gently, uncovered, for about 30 minutes until the onions have softened and turned a darker colour. Stir regularly to prevent the sugar burning on the bottom. Add the vinegar, red wine and jelly, and season with the salt and pepper. Cook for a further 20 to 30 minutes until most liquid has evaporated. By now it should be quite thick and syrupy.

To make the choux pastry, put the butter and water into a pan and bring slowly to the boil. Sift the flour and salt on to a sheet of greaseproof paper. Immediately the water boils, pull the pan off the heat and tip in the flour and salt using the paper as a chute. Beat the flour into the liquid as fast as you can until you have a rather rubbery-looking dough that leaves the sides of the pan clean. Tip it on to a cold plate, spread it out and allow to cool. When cooled, tip into a mixing bowl and, preferably using an electric whisk, beat in the eggs a little at a time until you have a shiny batter.

Heat the oven to 200°C/gas 6. Line a baking sheet with baking parchment.

Recipe continued overleaf

Recipe continued

Using 2 teaspoons, spoon small balls of batter on to the sheet. Leave a gap between them as they will puff up on cooking. Bake for about 20 minutes until well risen and golden.

Remove from the oven, make a small hole with a chopstick or skewer in the side of each one and return to the oven for a further 5 minutes to allow the steam to escape and to dry out the insides. When ready, remove to a wire rack to cool.

While cooling, make the horseradish cream by mixing all the ingredients together.

Brush the steak on both sides with oil and season with salt and pepper. In a frying or griddle pan over high heat, cook the steak for about 1½ minutes each side for rare, 2½ for medium rare, 3 for medium. Allow to rest for a couple of minutes before slicing into about 25 slices.

Assemble the canapés just before serving. Slice the choux buns through the middle horizontally. Spoon some of the red onion marmalade on the bottom layer, cover with a slice of steak, top with horseradish cream and a rocket or watercress leaf, then replace the top of the bun. Serve at once.

KELEMIA
SHALLOTS STUFFED WITH LAMB, CINNAMON & PINENUTS

=== SERVES FOUR AS A STARTER/MEZZE ===

In Thessaloniki I was always looking for recipes that reflected the connection between northern Greece and Turkey, and in particular dishes with a Byzantine flavour. I think this connection is what makes the cooking of Greek Macedonia so special. I ate this mezze of shallots stuffed with lamb, chilli, cinnamon, cumin and pine nuts at a lovely little restaurant near the White Tower called, a tad unoriginally, the Hellenic, i.e. the Greek. *Recipe photograph overleaf*

8 large banana shallots
350g minced lamb
½ tsp paprika
¼ tsp chilli flakes
1 tsp cumin seeds,
   toasted and ground
1 tsp ground cinnamon
2 tomatoes, skinned,
   roughly chopped
1½ tbsp tomato paste
30g pine nuts, toasted
Handful flat-leaf
   parsley, chopped
Pinch sugar
2 large cloves garlic,
   finely chopped or grated
½ tsp salt
5 turns black peppermill
1 tbsp white wine vinegar
3 tbsp olive oil
Pinch cayenne pepper

Bring a pan of water to the boil. Top and tail the shallots and peel them. Take each one and slit it open lengthways, cutting all the way down but only halfway through to the centre. Lower into the boiling water and cook for 7 to 8 minutes until the flesh starts to soften and the layers to separate. Drain and refresh under cold running water until cool enough to handle. Separate the layers, reserving the larger outer ones. Chop the small inner ones and keep them for the filling.

In a bowl, combine the lamb with the spices, tomato, tomato paste, reserved chopped onions, pine nuts, parsley (reserve a tablespoon for serving), sugar, garlic, salt and pepper. Fill each layer of shallot flesh with a spoonful of the mixture and roll up to encase the filling.

Pack the stuffed rolls into a flameproof casserole and pour over the vinegar and olive oil. Cover with a tight-fitting lid or foil and cook over medium-low heat for about 20 minutes.

Heat the oven to 200°C/gas 6.

Transfer the shallot rolls to the oven and bake, uncovered, for a further 15 to 20 minutes or until caramelized and golden. Serve with the pan juices spooned over and scatter with the reserved parsley and a pinch of cayenne pepper.

BAKED FETA CHEESE WITH TOMATO, RED PEPPER & CHILLIES

SERVES SIX

If you are like me, you need to build up on your repertoire of nibbles. These days I like to have a lot of people round for dinner at once, twelve or thirteen guests, and rather than a first course I set a table with prosciutto, marinated salmon, sliced tomatoes, salami, and something like this *bouyiourdi*. I leave a pile of thinly sliced baguette or similar biscuits for people to dip while they are sloshing back the champers. It's a great idea as it makes everything pleasingly informal.

200g feta cheese,
    broken into chunks
3 large ripe tomatoes,
    roughly chopped
½ red pepper, diced
3 pickled chillies, sliced
Pinch chilli flakes
½ tbsp dried Greek oregano
Freshly ground black pepper
3 tbsp olive oil, plus extra
    for greasing
50g kasseri/provolone/
    Gruyère cheese, grated
Flatbreads or toasted pita,
    to serve

Heat the oven to 200°C/gas 6. Grease a small baking dish with olive oil.

In a large bowl roughly combine all the ingredients except the olive oil and grated cheese. Tip into the greased dish. Drizzle with olive oil, sprinkle over the grated cheese and bake for about 20 minutes until the top is golden and bubbling. Cool for 5 minutes before serving with flatbreads or pita.

BOLINHOS DE BACALHAU
SALT COD FRITTERS
MAKES EIGHTEEN TO TWENTY

I bought two or three of these at Lisbon airport as we were leaving and was astounded how good they were, at an airport indeed. They are made with salt cod and potato, and what makes them special is the high percentage of fish to potato, and also the fact that it is salt fish. Normally you wouldn't dream of putting so much salt with fresh fish, everybody would complain, but as a traditional product it is perfectly OK and even lovely because of it. Also, once salted it stands up to being reheated far better. If you are going to make these as a nibbles dish, you need have no qualms about making and frying them in the morning and reheating them on an oven tray just before opening the champagne.

400g salt cod (dry weight)
400ml milk
350g floury potatoes
   in their skins
1 tsp olive oil
1 small onion,
   coarsely chopped
2 cloves garlic,
   roughly chopped
Small handful flat-leaf
   parsley, chopped
Small handful coriander,
   chopped
8 turns black peppermill
1 egg, beaten
600ml sunflower oil

To serve
2 lemons, cut into wedges
Olives

Soak the cod in cold water for 24 hours, changing the water 3 or 4 times and discarding.

Rinse the cod, put it in a saucepan, cover with the milk and bring to the boil, then turn down to a simmer and cook until tender, about 15 minutes.

Boil the potatoes until tender, about 15 to 20 minutes. Drain and cool a little before slipping off the skins, then mash the potato until fluffy.

Remove the cod from the milk and allow to cool. Remove any skin and bones and put the cod into a food processor with the oil, onion and garlic and pulse to a paste. In a large bowl mix the paste with the mashed potato, herbs, pepper and egg. The mixture should be quite stiff. Using 2 dessertspoons, quenelle the mixture into rugby-ball shapes and set aside.

Heat the oil in a large, heavy pan to 165°C, using a temperature probe or sugar thermometer to check. Place a plate lined with kitchen paper next to the pan. Fry the fritters in small batches for 2 to 3 minutes until rich golden brown. Remove with a slotted spoon and drain on the lined plate. Serve immediately with lemon wedges and olives. Alternatively, set aside now to reheat in the oven (10 to 12 minutes at 160°C/gas 3) when guests arrive.

RISSÓIS DE CAMARÃO
PRAWN FRIED DUMPLINGS
MAKES FIFTY TO SIXTY

These are a must for nibbles, absolutely a must. *Recipe photograph overleaf*

For the dough
500ml full-fat milk
60g butter
1 tsp fine salt
285g plain flour

For the filling
30g butter
1 small onion,
    finely chopped
30g plain flour
250ml milk
1 tbsp finely chopped
    coriander
Pinch chilli flakes
½ tsp fine salt
6 turns black peppermill
400g raw prawns, peeled,
    deveined, chopped into
    pea-sized pieces

To finish
1 litre rapeseed
    or vegetable oil
3 large eggs, beaten
250g dried white
    Breadcrumbs (page 309)

Put the milk, butter and salt in a large saucepan and heat until the butter is melted. Sift the flour on to a sheet of greaseproof paper. Take the pan off the heat and add the flour all at once, using the paper as a chute. Beat vigorously until the dough leaves the sides of the pan. Turn the dough on to a lightly floured work surface and knead until silky and smooth. Divide into two pieces and set aside to cool and rest.

For the filling, melt the butter in a saucepan over medium heat. Add the onion and fry gently until softened, about 5 to 10 minutes. Add the flour and cook for 1 minute, then gradually add the milk and keep stirring until the sauce is thick. Stir in the coriander, chilli flakes, salt and pepper. Stir in the chopped raw prawns and set aside to cool. (The prawns will cook when the pastry is deep-fried.)

Take one piece of the dough and roll out to 3mm thick. Use an 8cm pastry cutter to cut out discs. Spoon a teaspoonful of filling into the centre of each disc and fold the dough over into a semicircle, pinching the edges to contain the filling. Do the same with the remainder of the dough, until the filling is all used up.

Heat the oven to 100°C/gas ¼. Heat the oil in a large, heavy pan to 175°C, using a temperature probe or sugar thermometer to check. Place a plate lined with kitchen paper alongside the hob.

Dip each dumpling in the beaten egg, then the breadcrumbs, and fry a few at a time for 3 to 4 minutes until browned all over. Remove with a slotted spoon and drain on kitchen paper, then keep warm in the oven while you cook the rest. Serve warm.

CHICHARRONES DE CÁDIZ
SLICED BELLY PORK *WITH* SMOKED PAPRIKA & CUMIN SEEDS

SERVES ABOUT TWENTY

I took my three sons, Ed, Jack and Charlie, for a recce to Cadiz a few months back. I had a suspicion that chicharrones would feature highly in a list of their best dishes, and it did. I also singled out a tapas bar called Casa Manteca – 'the Lard'. There has to be something special about a bar named after a lump of fat. Of course, the bar was named for the very thinly sliced, marinated and confited belly pork that they serve on sheets of greaseproof paper. To us, the bar was heaven. The slices came sprinkled with sea salt and lemon juice, and the beer, Cruzcampo, we ordered in tiny, ice-cold glasses. Rest assured, not just a single round of tiny glasses, but many, many rounds of tiny glasses. The chicharrones and the cold beer and the paintings, pictures and posters of bullfighters all round filled us with joy and wonder at the machismo of Spain. The tapas bar in Spain is one of life's delights.

2kg pork belly,
   skinned and boned
2 tbsp sea salt,
   plus extra to serve
Freshly ground black pepper
5 cloves garlic,
   grated or crushed
2 tbsp sweet smoked paprika
   (*pimentón dulce*)
1 tbsp fennel seeds
1 tbsp dried oregano
750g lard, melted

To serve
Juice 1 lemon
Sea salt
1 tsp cumin seeds,
   toasted and ground
Mojo picón (page 308)

Rub the pork belly all over with sea salt and pepper, place in a bowl and cover with clingfilm. Refrigerate for 24 hours. After this time, brush off any excess salt and throw away any liquid that has been drawn out of the meat.

Heat the oven to 130°C/gas 1.

Pat the meat dry with kitchen paper and rub in the garlic, *pimentón*, fennel seeds and oregano, massaging into the meat. Place the meat in an ovenproof dish for which you have a tight-fitting lid, and add the melted lard. Dampen a piece of greaseproof paper large enough to cover the dish, scrunch it up to make it pliable, then smooth it out. Cover the meat and fat well with the paper and put on the lid. Bake for about 2 to 2½ hours until the meat is tender. It should not be falling apart – you want to be able to slice it thinly – so check after about 2 hours.

Remove from the oven, uncover and allow to cool. When cool, take the pork from the lard, wrap in foil or clingfilm, place on a board and press down with another board and a weight. Transfer to the fridge. (Keep the leftover lard in a jam jar and eat it spread on bread.)

Store until ready to serve, on sheets of greaseproof paper, sliced very thinly and sprinkled with lemon juice, sea salt and freshly ground cumin, or with the *Mojo picón* sauce. Both the pork and the lard keep for up to 2 weeks in the fridge.

FAVA SANTORINI
PURÉE OF SPLIT YELLOW PEAS WITH GARLIC, THYME, RED ONION & CAPERS

=== SERVES FOUR ===

I don't know why I have never come across Fava Santorini before, not even in Santorini. It was with great enthusiasm that I tried this fava bean hummus in Thessaloniki, finished with sliced red onion and capers. It was almost a revelation, it was that good. Though it's called fava, it is made with yellow split peas, the best of which come from the bucket-list island of Santorini. It's because a significant minority of Mediterranean people suffer from an allergy to broad beans, called favism. Yellow split peas make a good substitute.

100ml olive oil,
  plus extra to serve
1 large onion,
  roughly chopped
2 cloves garlic, chopped
Sprig thyme
500g yellow split
  peas, rinsed
1.2 litres water
1 small red onion,
  finely sliced
1 tbsp brown sugar
Juice 1 lemon
Salt and freshly ground
  black pepper
1 tbsp capers, drained
Small handful flat-leaf
  parsley, chopped

Heat 2 tablespoons of the olive oil in a large pan over medium heat, add the onion, garlic and thyme, and sweat until soft and translucent, 5 to 10 minutes.

Add the split peas. Pour in the water, bring up to the boil and skim off any white scum that may appear on the surface, then turn the heat down and simmer gently with a lid on the pan for about 45 to 60 minutes, until the split peas are thick and mushy.

In a separate pan, heat 1 tablespoon of the olive oil over a very low heat. Add the red onion and sugar and gently caramelize for about 15 to 20 minutes until the onion has taken on a brown colour and a soft melting texture. Increase the heat for the last couple of minutes to gain more colour.

Add the remaining olive oil and the lemon juice to the peas. Using a food processor or a stick blender, pulse to a coarse purée, not too smooth. Season to taste with salt and pepper. Serve the fava with a drizzle more olive oil, scattered with the caramelized red onion, capers and parsley.

PANELLE ALLA CECI
CHICKPEA AND FENNEL
SEED FRITTERS

SERVES FOUR

When I first heard about these I was not overenthusiastic. Chickpea fritters in white bread buns don't sound too wonderful. However, on the streets of Palermo, fresh from the fryer, is a different matter altogether, and having made them a couple of times I think they are well worth making back home too. The combination of gram flour and fennel seeds gives them a delightfully Middle Eastern twist.

Recipe photograph overleaf

750ml very cold water
250g chickpea (gram) flour
1 tsp fennel seeds, ground
1 tsp salt
8 turns black peppermill
Handful flat-leaf parsley, chopped
100ml olive oil, for frying

To serve
4 white bread rolls
Juice 1 lemon
Sea salt

Pour the water into a large saucepan. Using a balloon whisk, pour in the gram flour in a steady stream and whisk to avoid lumps. Once the flour is incorporated and has formed a paste, add the fennel seeds.

Heat the pan and gradually bring up to a boil, stirring all the time, making sure it doesn't catch on the bottom. Turn down to a simmer and keep stirring for about 10 to 15 minutes until thick: the paste should leave the sides of the pan clean.

Take off the heat and stir in the salt, pepper and parsley. Spoon the mixture into a small loaf tin (about 450g) lined with clingfilm and allow to cool completely.

When cold, turn out and slice fairly thinly. Shallow-fry for a couple of minutes each side until crisp and golden around the edges. Pile 3 or 4 slices in a roll sprinkled with lemon juice and a little salt.

SALMOREJO
CHILLED TOMATO SOUP
WITH SERRANO HAM & TUNA FLAKES

SERVES SIX TO EIGHT AS A STARTER

If you have a greenhouse and a glut of tomatoes, or if you are renting a villa somewhere and the ones in the shop down the road are particularly cheap and lovely, this is the soup for you. Don't bother with the dish if you only have watery supermarket tomatoes. What I really like about this are the *guarniciones*, in this case chopped hard-boiled eggs, serrano ham, tuna flakes, onion, chopped green pepper and a pinch of *peperoncini* for good measure. As well as the best, ripest, tastiest tomatoes, good sherry vinegar is also crucial to this dish.

1kg ripe large tomatoes,
  skinned, cored
2 cloves garlic,
  roughly chopped
2 slices (about 80–100g)
  stale white country bread
  or sourdough, soaked
  in water and excess
  squeezed out
125ml extra-virgin olive oil
½–1 tsp salt
2 tbsp sherry vinegar

*For the garnishes
  (guarniciones)*
2 hard-boiled eggs, chopped
2 tbsp tuna flakes
½ small onion, finely chopped
50g serrano ham, chopped
½ green pepper,
  finely chopped
Peperoncini (chilli flakes)

Put the tomatoes and garlic in a food processor and blitz until smooth. Add the soaked bread, 100ml of the olive oil and salt to taste. Pulse again and add enough water to give a smooth and creamy soup. Add the sherry vinegar and pulse again to combine. Check the seasoning, adding more salt if required. Chill thoroughly before serving.

Serve in cold bowls, drizzled with the remaining olive oil, with the *guarniciones* alongside.

SFINCIONE
SICILIAN PIZZA

This is the ultimate topping for a freshly baked focaccia. Little *sfincione* stalls exist all over Palermo. It couldn't be simpler or more delicious, or cheaper – about two euros for an enormous slab served on greaseproof paper. *Recipe photograph overleaf*

For the dough
1 tbsp dried yeast
1 tsp caster sugar
400–450ml warm water
675g strong white flour,
    plus extra for dusting
1 tsp salt
90ml olive oil, plus extra
    for greasing
1 tbsp polenta, for baking

For the tomato sauce
2 tbsp olive oil
2 cloves garlic, finely
    chopped or grated
500g fresh tomatoes
    or 1 x 400g tin plus
    1 tsp sugar
½ tsp salt
6–8 turns black peppermill

For the toppings
5 tbsp olive oil
3 large onions, sliced
1 tsp dried oregano
8 anchovy fillets from a tin
50g pecorino, grated
30g dried white *Breadcrumbs*
    (page 309)
Pinch chilli flakes (optional)
6–8 turns black peppermill

Mix the dried yeast with the sugar and a few tablespoons of the measured water and leave for about 5 minutes to activate. Put the flour and salt in a food mixer, add the frothy yeast, 400ml of the measured water and the olive oil and mix with a dough hook for 1 to 2 minutes. It should show signs of becoming a soft dough. If dry, add more of the water. Continue mixing for about 5 minutes until you have a smooth, elastic dough. If you don't have a food mixer with a dough hook, then turn out on to a lightly floured surface and knead by hand for about 8 minutes.

Roll the dough into a ball, place in an oiled bowl, cover the bowl with cling film and set aside at room temperature until doubled in size: 1 to 2 hours.

Make the tomato sauce. Heat the olive oil in a pan over medium heat and add the garlic. After 1 to 2 minutes, add the tomatoes. Simmer, breaking up with a wooden spoon, until reduced and thickened, about 15 to 20 minutes. Whizz in a blender, season with the salt and pepper and set aside.

For the toppings, warm the olive oil in a pan over low heat and add the sliced onions. Cover and cook gently for 20 to 30 minutes until golden and meltingly soft. Take the lid off the pan for the final 5 minutes to allow any excess liquid to evaporate.

Heat the oven to 220°C/gas 7.

Punch the risen dough down and turn out on to a lightly floured board. Lightly oil a rectangular baking tray about 25cm x 35cm and dust with the polenta. Roll out the dough, place it in the tray and stretch it into the corners. Allow to rise again for 25 to 30 minutes at room temperature, covered with a tea towel.

Spread with tomato sauce (freeze any remainder), then add the onions, oregano and anchovies. Mix the pecorino with the breadcrumbs and sprinkle over the surface. Season with chilli, if you like, and black pepper. Bake for 25 to 30 minutes, reducing the temperature to 200°C/gas 6 after the first 5 minutes. Allow to cool a little before serving.

HALIBUT SOUP
WITH CREAM, APPLE & DILL
=== SERVES FOUR ===

Gísli Matthías Auðunsson, the chef at Matur og Drykkur ('Food and Drink'), is part of a new breed of young Icelandic cooks who are beginning to change Icelandic cuisine, rather in the way that René Redzipi in Copenhagen did, and I say this because Iceland and Denmark were one and the same for hundreds of years. This recipe is based on a dish of his grandmother's but with twenty-first-century additions. It is not a dish to cook every day, but it is worth putting in the effort, even down to the dill oil. Feel free to use fish other than halibut, since outside Icelandic waters it's a threatened species, though Pacific halibut is available in the UK and is excellent, and it is possible to buy farmed halibut too. I suggest hake or even cod as a substitute.

2 tbsp vegetable oil
2 banana shallots, sliced
3 bay leaves
4 sprigs thyme
2½ tbsp butter
100ml white wine
200ml *Fish stock* (page 307)
Pinch pink peppercorns
1 Bramley apple
1 tbsp *Dill oil* (page 309)
200ml single cream
½ tsp salt
Juice ½ lemon
125g unsalted butter
250g fillet of halibut,
    skinned and cut
    into small chunks
4 tbsp chopped mixed
    raisins and dates

Heat the vegetable oil in a pan over medium heat, add the shallots and soften for a few minutes. Add the bay leaves, thyme, butter and white wine and reduce by half. Add the fish stock and cook for about 5 minutes, then add the peppercorns. Peel the apple and add the peel to the soup. Chop the apple flesh and cover it with dill oil.

Continue to cook the soup for a further 10 minutes, then add the single cream and cook for 2 to 3 minutes. Pass through a sieve, return to a clean or rinsed-out pan, season with salt and lemon juice, and whisk in the 125g butter. Add the halibut to the creamy soup and cook for a few minutes until opaque.

In each bowl put a tablespoon of the chopped raisins and dates. Divide the apple in dill oil between the bowls, then spoon the fish and its soup on top. Serve straight away.

SASHIMI

SERVES FOUR

In the central market in Cadiz is a sushi and sashimi stall called Gadisushi, run by Mauricio Navascués. He has been to Japan but learnt to make sushi mainly with his friends in Cadiz, and he says that after four years he is still learning. His raw material, bluefin tuna, is certainly as good as you get in the Tsukiji fish market in Tokyo. The majority of the tuna from Cadiz gets exported to Japan, but there is plenty to go round in Cadiz in the tuna season. It was very interesting how busy the stall was with locals when I was there, though I was slightly interrupted while enjoying my sashimi by a seemingly constant stream of British cruise-ship passengers who recognized me from the TV.

180g salmon fillet,
    skinned and pin-boned
180g yellowtail tuna fillet

For the Tosa sauce
250ml soy sauce
5cm piece kombu
3 tbsp mirin
Small handful bonito flakes

*For the wakame
    seaweed salad*
25g dried chopped wakame
    seaweed, mixed dried
    seaweed or Hiyasha
    wakame (available via
    online stores/Asian
    supermarkets)
1 tbsp mirin
1 tbsp rice wine vinegar
1 tbsp dark soy sauce
1 tbsp toasted sesame oil
½ red chilli, finely chopped
1 heaped tsp sesame seeds

To serve
Wasabi
Pickled sushi ginger

To make the Tosa sauce, combine all the ingredients and leave for 24 hours, then strain. This will keep for up to a year.

For the salad, rehydrate the dried seaweed for about 5 minutes in cold water, then drain well. Mix together the mirin, rice wine vinegar, dark soy sauce and sesame oil and dress the seaweed with it. Stir through the chilli and sesame seeds.

Carefully trim the brown/grey-coloured meat from the skinned side of the salmon fillet and cut both the salmon and tuna across the grain into 7mm-thick slices.

Serve the sashimi with a small dipping bowl of the Tosa sauce, a hazelnut-sized amount of wasabi, a heap of the seaweed salad and a teaspoon of pickled sushi ginger alongside.

OCTOPUS SALAD *WITH* RED ONION, GARLIC & PARSLEY

SERVES FOUR TO SIX

This is far and away the most popular salad in Portugal, let alone Lisbon. It is simple, a perfect example of 'less is more'. One and a half kilos of whole octopus will serve about four to six as a starter, but if you want to use the same quantity for, say, eight people, add 300g sliced new potatoes. It's important to get the right octopus for this, usually Spanish or Portuguese *Octopus vulgaris*, and it's perfectly in order to use from frozen. *Recipe photograph overleaf*

Salt
1.5kg uncooked octopus,
    gutted, eyes and beak
    removed, cleaned
1 onion, halved
3 bay leaves

For the salad
1 small red onion,
    finely chopped
2 cloves garlic, grated
Large handful coriander or
    flat-leaf parsley, chopped
90ml olive oil
35ml white wine vinegar
½–1 tsp sea salt flakes
6 turns black peppermill

Bring a large pan of salted water (1 teaspoon salt per 600ml water) to the boil. Put in the prepared octopus with the onion and bay leaves and simmer for at least 45 and up to 60 minutes until tender. Drain the octopus and allow to cool. Cut the body and tentacles into chunks of about 2.5cm.

In a large bowl, mix the octopus with the onion, garlic and coriander or parsley, and dress with the olive oil, vinegar and salt and pepper. Let the salad marinate for 20 to 30 minutes in the dressing before serving.

The salad can be made a day in advance and kept covered in the fridge. Remove an hour before serving to bring up to room temperature.

CALDILLO DE PEROS
SOUP OF HAKE *with* SEVILLE ORANGES & SAFFRON

This is a simple and unusual fish soup which combines the following ingredients: Seville oranges, saffron, sherry vinegar, tomato, garlic and dried bread. You have to be prepared for the bitterness of the oranges, normally only encountered in marmalade. I think bitter is an important and underrated element in our cooking. It combines especially well with a beautiful and similarly undervalued fish like hake. One of the I things I love about Spanish cooking is the *picada*. This is a means of thickening a soup or stew by blending some of the ingredients with dried bread then stirring it back into the dish. I suggest using stale sourdough, perhaps even giving a little toasting first.

1.5 litres *Fish stock*
    (see page 307)
1 Seville orange, zest pared
    with a sharp knife or potato
    peeler and juice reserved
1 large ripe tomato,
    skinned and halved
1 large onion, cut in half
3 parsley stalks
1 clove garlic, peeled
    but left whole
1 slice stale white bread,
    preferably sourdough,
    broken into chunks
Pinch saffron threads
2 tsp sherry vinegar
600g skinned hake fillet,
    cut into 3cm pieces
Salt
Pinch sugar
Few chives, chopped
    for garnish

In a large pan, heat the fish stock, orange zest, tomato, onion and parsley stalks and bring to a boil, then turn down to a simmer and cook for 15 minutes. Strain the stock into another saucepan. Discard the orange zest and parsley and set the vegetables aside.

In a small dry frying pan, toast the clove of garlic, for a couple of minutes, or until browned on all sides. Remove from the heat.

In a blender or food processor, mix 200ml of the fish stock with the cooked tomato, and onion, add the roasted garlic, bread pieces, saffron and vinegar. Blend to a smooth purée. Mix with the remaining stock, return to the saucepan and bring to a gentle simmer. Add the hake pieces to the pan. Turn the heat right down and gently poach the fish for about 5 minutes or until the fish turns opaque.

Remove from the heat, taste and season with salt. Add the bitter orange juice and sugar, stir and let it sit for 5 minutes. Ladle into warmed bowls and sprinkle with snipped chives.

MONKFISH FRITTERS WITH CUMIN, GARLIC & PIMENTÓN

SERVES FOUR AS A STARTER

Adobo is a cumin- and oregano-flavoured marinade for both pork and fish, the most popular fish in Cadiz being dogfish. I felt quite nostalgic wandering through the Mercado de Abastos, seeing piles of whole dogfish, both smooth hounds and lesser and greater spotted. In the 1970s, lots of Padstow lobster fishermen used to go fishing for dogfish in the winter months when it was too rough for shellfish. These days you don't see them much as they were overfished. I have written this recipe for firm-textured monkfish instead.

400g monkfish
2 tbsp olive oil
1 tbsp sherry vinegar
1 tbsp water
1 clove garlic, grated
½ tsp sweet smoked paprika
    (*pimentón dulce*)
½ tsp dried oregano
10 turns black peppermill
½ tsp salt
1 tsp cumin seeds
100g semolina
200ml olive oil, for frying

To serve
1 lemon, cut into wedges
Mustard mayonnaise
    (page 308)

Cut the fish into 4cm cubes, discarding any skin and bone. Put in a glass or ceramic bowl. Mix together the oil, vinegar, water, garlic, paprika, oregano, pepper, salt and half the cumin seeds. Pour over the fish and mix well. Marinate for at least 2 hours.

Drain the fish well, dredge in semolina and fry the pieces a few at a time in hot olive oil until golden and crisp. Drain on paper towel and serve hot, sprinkled with the remaining cumin seeds. Serve with lemon wedges, and mayonnaise on the side.

TORTELLINI IN BRODO

The first rule I would say about making tortellini from Bologna is to invest in some eggs with good, deep-yellow yolks. Burford browns are the ones to go for. The pasta was so bright yellow in colour that I was moved to think they'd added food dye, but I learnt a very embarrassing lesson fifteen years ago when I suggested that my farmer neighbour George Trenouth in Trevone had added yellow colouring to his butter. This was in May, when the pasture was so green that the cows could not help but produce milk that led to butter of that hue. The same is true, I am sure, of Bologna, where they have very contented, well-fed chickens. The filling, a mixture of minced pork and mortadella, prosciutto and nutmeg, is so special. You can make up a lot of these; they freeze very well, as does the brodo.

For the filling
30g butter
120g minced pork
50g Parmesan cheese,
    grated, plus extra to serve
150g prosciutto, chopped
150g mortadella, chopped
1 egg
Salt and freshly ground
    black pepper
Few rasps freshly
    grated nutmeg

For the brodo
300g shin of beef
500g beef bones
300g chicken thighs
    and drumsticks, skin on
1 small onion, halved
2 sticks celery,
    roughly chopped
1 carrot, roughly chopped
1 sprig thyme

For the pasta
400g 00 pasta flour,
    plus extra for dusting
1 tsp salt
4 eggs, beaten

Make the brodo by placing all the ingredients in a large pan or stockpot. Cover with about 3 litres of water, or more if necessary to cover the meat and bones. Bring to the boil, skim off any scum and then simmer for 3 to 4 hours. When ready, strain through a fine sieve or a sieve lined with a muslin and reserve until ready to use. Discard the vegetables, meat and bones.

Make the pasta by combining the flour, salt and eggs in a food processor to 'breadcrumb' stage, then tip out on to a lightly floured board and knead for 3 to 4 minutes until smooth and elastic. Form into a ball, wrap in clingfilm and allow to rest for at least 30 minutes before rolling.

For the filling, heat the butter in a pan and fry the pork until browned. Transfer to a bowl to cool before adding the remaining ingredients. Season to taste with salt, pepper and nutmeg and blitz in a food processor to a paste.

Roll the pasta into sheets about 2–3mm thick using a rolling pin or pasta machine. Cut into 5cm squares. Put a scant teaspoonful of filling into the centre of each square. Fold the pasta corner to corner to make a triangle with the filling encased. Press to seal the edges, then wrap each triangle around your little finger and pinch the points together. Curl the uppermost point backwards to give the classic tortellini shape.

To serve, heat the brodo until boiling and taste for seasoning. Cook the tortellini for about 3 minutes, then serve the pasta in a bowl with a ladle or two of the brodo and sprinkled generously with Parmesan cheese.

PIAZ
SALAD OF CANNELLINI BEANS, RED ONIONS, PEPPERS AND TOMATOES

SERVES EIGHT TO TEN

As I have said elsewhere, if you really want to understand how great Greek cuisine can be, you need to go to Thessaloniki. This salad appears in the autumn in many restaurants there, though this particular version comes from To Elliniko in Kallari Street. It's just a lovely bean salad with tomatoes, red pepper, chilli and oregano, great with grilled meat or fish.

500g dried cannellini beans,
   soaked overnight
4 tbsp olive oil
Juice 1 lemon
Handful flat-leaf parsley,
   chopped
1 red onion, halved
   and finely sliced
1 red pepper, deseeded
   and chopped
2 large ripe tomatoes,
   skinned, coarsely chopped
1 tsp dried oregano
1½–2 tsp salt
8 turns black peppermill
4–6 pickled chillies, whole,
   to serve

Drain the soaked beans, rinse, put in a pan and cover with fresh water. Bring up to the boil and boil for 10 minutes, skimming off any white scum that rises to the surface. Turn down the heat and simmer for about an hour or until tender but not mushy. Drain, set aside and allow to cool completely.

In a large bowl mix the beans with the olive oil, lemon juice, parsley, onion, red pepper, tomatoes, oregano, salt and pepper. Serve with pickled chillies on the side.

SALAD OF GRILLED TOMATOES
WITH ROCKET & BALSAMIC VINEGAR

SERVES THREE TO SIX

Before going to Thessaloniki I had heard that it was possibly the best city on Greece for food. I was not disappointed. Not only is there great Greek and Turkish food, but also a thriving restaurant culture, featuring dishes that are certainly Greek in influence but refreshingly innovative. This recipe comes from Xontro Alati where they have taken gloriously voluptuous Greek beef tomatoes for a salad, then actually grilled them, only enough until they are soft, and sprinkled them with salt, vinegar, Kalamata olives and olive oil. Maybe it doesn't seem much, but these tomatoes with rocket leaves made a perfect salad for me, with a souvlaki. It is one of the dishes where the quality of the tomatoes is essential, so don't bother until late summer.

Recipe photograph overleaf

6 large vine tomatoes, peeled
Olive oil
150g rocket, washed
Balsamic vinegar
Salt
12 Kalamata olives

Heat a grill to medium. Cut the peeled tomatoes in half horizontally, drizzle with a little olive oil and grill for 5 to 10 minutes until warmed through and starting to soften. Arrange on a bed of rocket leaves and dress with olive oil, balsamic vinegar and salt. Scatter the Kalamata olives over the top and serve.

SATURDAY NIGHT MAINS

CÔTE DE BOEUF OR ENTRECÔTE STEAK WITH BORDELAISE SAUCE 184

DUCK & PORCINI PITHIVIER WITH RED WINE & ARMAGNAC 185

LEMON SOLE WITH POINTED CABBAGE & LEMON BUTTER SAUCE 190

CHEFFY SOLE A LA MEUNIERE 194

VIENNESE GULASCH WITH SPÄTZLE 195

WIENER SCHNITZEL WITH VIENNESE POTATO SALAD 198

SEARED TUNA WITH RED WINE, OLIVE OIL & AROMATIC HERBS 200

BAKED SEA BREAM ROTA-STYLE 201

VEAL & PORK DUMPLINGS WITH BEETROOT & TABASCO 204

DUCK RAGÙ WITH TAGLIATELLE 205

PORK BELLY SLICES WITH PARSLEY SAUCE & LOVAGE POTATOES 208

SICILIAN FRITELLA RISOTTO 209

PETZ'S SPICED CABBAGE WITH SMOKED HAM 213

There is nothing I enjoy more in life than cooking. I don't mind the hard work it entails, and as for guests, the more the merrier for me. There is nothing quite like the challenge of cooking something memorable for your friends on a Saturday night. The trick, though – and I find this so much with disappointing dinners made by famous chefs out of the comfort zones of their own kitchens, cooking for a function or a special dinner – is not to try to be *too* memorable. Long ago an Austrian ski instructor made the simple observation of my skiing style: you think too much. The remedy: don't think so much. It's the same with cooking. Another way of putting it is this: keep it simple, stupid. I am only saying this because I endlessly dream of the most wonderful food imaginable, all cooked at the last minute, and I know this has nothing to do with the reality of time, space, defects in equipment, punctuality of guests, forgetting the peas, or the inadvisability of a glass or two of wine twenty minutes before everybody arrives.

So with these things in mind, let me suggest three of the dishes in this chapter and give you some information about timing. First, the Duck Ragù with Tagliatelle on page 205. It goes without saying that only one part of this dish should be cooked at the last minute: the pasta. The ragù itself needs to have been finished that morning at the latest. Even the Parmesan to sprinkle over the finished dish can be grated in advance. The pasta should be made that morning, so the completion of the dish is simply boiling the pasta for 4 to 5 minutes in plenty of salted water. And take the côte de boeuf option in Steak with Bordelaise Sauce on page 184. It's unwise to show off the cooking of a côte de boeuf on a barbecue if you want to produce the most perfectly cooked piece of meat. Things can go wrong. Among them, in my experience, too many helpful suggestions from the group of men with beers standing around the barbecue. OK, so it doesn't really matter if everything is a bit overcooked or a bit black but, if you want perfection, cook the côte(s) at a quiet time for about 8 minutes on each side, concentrating on a perfect grilled look, and finish the chops in your oven before your guests arrive, allowing at least half an hour for the meat to rest. Finally, the Viennese Gulasch with Spätzle on page 195. Gulasch is always better reheated from the previous day, so do that. The spätzle can be made and cooked earlier, then all you need to do is to toss them in foaming butter and nutmeg just before you serve. Simple as building blocks – but where *does* the time go?

CÔTE DE BOEUF OR ENTRECÔTE STEAK WITH BORDELAISE SAUCE

SERVES FOUR

After a couple of days in Bordeaux, you begin to see that the red wines of the region were made specifically to go with the beef. I don't believe there is a better match on earth. And from a country that invented haute cuisine it's wonderful to realize that the simpler the preparation and cooking of the beef, the better the match with the wine.

I was lucky enough to have a côte de boeuf cooked for me on the lawn of Château Phélan Ségur. The barbecue was fired with vine prunings, not just any old vine prunings, but ones that had been used in the fermentation vats to weigh down all the solid material and were therefore a delicate shade of purple. The chef assured me that this improved the flavour of the beef, and I willingly agreed that it did when I tasted the most delicious meat, which came from ten-year-old-plus cows and heifers from Bazas.

The finishing touch was to coat the surface with beef marrow and sear it with a red-hot poker. This is not something that anyone can easily reproduce outside the area, so there follows a simple recipe for entrecôte steak with Bordelaise sauce. Serve with chips, green beans and red wine. *Recipe photograph overleaf*

1 beef marrow bone,
　cut into 4 x 8cm pieces
Salt and freshly ground
　black pepper
Olive oil
4 entrecote steaks, each
　200–225g and 3–4cm thick
2 tsp sunflower or
　rapeseed oil

For the Bordelaise sauce
125ml claret (red wine)
1 shallot, finely chopped
Sprig thyme
1 bay leaf
250ml demi-glace or
　concentrated *Beef stock*
　(page 307)
30g unsalted cold
　butter, cubed
Pinch sugar, if required
Handful parsley, chopped

Heat the oven to 200°C/gas 6.

Place the marrow bones upright on a greased baking sheet. Season with salt and pepper and a splash of olive oil. Roast for about 10 minutes, until the marrow comes away from the bone. When cool enough to handle, scoop out the marrow, chop and set aside.

Get a frying pan really hot, brush the steak with the sunflower or rapeseed oil and season with salt and pepper. Fry the steaks in the pan for about 1½ minutes each side for rare, 2½ for medium rare, 3 minutes for medium. Once cooked to your preference, set aside to rest.

For the sauce, add the red wine to the pan along with the shallot, thyme and bay leaf and boil to reduce by about two-thirds, cleaning all the meat juices off the bottom of the pan. Add the beef stock and continue to cook for a couple of minutes, whisk in the cold butter and chopped marrow, taste and adjust for seasoning and, if required, add a pinch of sugar. Add the chopped parsley and any juices from the rested steak. Serve the steak with a spoonful of the sauce.

CÔTE DE BOEUF FOR TWO

To cook a côte de boeuf for two rather than individual steaks, here is how.

1 tbsp olive oil
60g butter
1kg double-cut côte
    de boeuf on the bone,
    at room temperature
Salt and freshly ground
    black pepper
2 sprigs fresh thyme

Heat the oven to 200°C/gas 6.

Warm an ovenproof pan over high heat and add the oil and butter. Season the côte de boeuf with salt and pepper, then sear for about 3 minutes on each side. Do not move it around, just allow it to sit in the hot pan to achieve a brown 'crust' on the outside. Then turn over and repeat. (This can also be done on a griddle pan or over hot coals on a barbecue.) Add the thyme to the pan under the meat, transfer to the oven and cook for 10 minutes for rare/medium-rare steaks. Remove from the oven and rest for 10 minutes. Traditionally côte de boeuf for two is served and carved at the table. Serve with the Bordelaise sauce and chips or Dauphinoise potatoes.

BARBECUE

Should you decide to cook a côte de boeuf on the barbecue, make the sauce in a large frying pan as described in the recipe, cut the barbecued côte de boeuf into 1cm slices, having first removed the bone, and put the slices and the bone on top of the Bordelaise sauce. Cover and leave to rest for 10 minutes, then serve.

DUCK & PORCINI PITHIVIER
WITH RED WINE & ARMAGNAC

=== SERVES SIX ===

This is a fabulous dish which we plan to showcase in our restaurant in Marlborough, opening this year. I got the idea when it was served as a 'modest' appetizer to the Côte du Boeuf on the lawn of Château Phélan Ségur (see page 184). All that remains is to point out that this recipe will make six individual pithiviers, or three to share between six.

---

2 duck breasts
   and 2 duck legs
3 medium onions (600g total),
   finely chopped
100g pancetta, very
   finely chopped
10g garlic, finely chopped
250g portobello
   mushrooms, sliced
15g dried porcini, soaked
   in about 60ml water
200g duck livers,
   thickly sliced
60ml red wine
50ml Armagnac
1 tbsp soy sauce
750ml dark strong-flavoured
   Chicken stock, or *Beef stock*
   (page 307)
1 tsp salt
Sprig thyme
1 bay leaf
1 tsp truffle oil
2 eggs, beaten
500g block puff pastry
Flour for dusting
2 egg yolks, beaten
   with a fork
20 turns black peppermill
50g butter

In a large, dry frying pan over medium heat, brown the duck skin-side down to render down its fat, about 10 minutes. Pour out and keep the fat, then brown the duck on the other side.

In a 4-litre saucepan or casserole over medium heat, fry the onion, pancetta and garlic in 3 tablespoons of the duck fat until brown, 5 to 10 minutes. Add the portobello and porcini mushrooms and livers, and stir until coloured, about 3 to 4 minutes. Add the duck, red wine, Armagnac and soy sauce, bring to the boil, then cook until reduced by three-quarters. Add the stock, salt, thyme and bay leaf and simmer for 45 minutes, covered with a lid, then remove the lid and cook for a further 15 minutes until the duck is tender and the liquid has reduced.

Pour off 175ml of the liquid and strain into a clean pan for the jus. Reduce the remaining liquid in the casserole until it coats the back of a spoon, then leave to cool. Remove the bones from the duck. Discard the bay leaf and thyme sprigs. Taste the mixture and adjust the seasoning; stir in the truffle oil and eggs.

Heat the oven to 200°C/gas 6.

On a lightly floured surface, roll out the puff pastry to about 4mm thick. Cut out either 12 small discs or 6 larger ones. Line 1 or 2 baking sheets with baking parchment and place 6 small or 3 large discs of pastry on them. Arrange the duck mixture on the pastry bases, leaving a border of about 3cm.

Brush the border of the pastry with a little egg yolk and drape the second disc of pastry over the filling. Crimp or twist the edges together. Make a small hole in the centre of the lid to allow steam to escape. With a sharp-bladed knife, score the lid like the curved spokes of a wheel. Brush with the egg yolk.

Bake for the larger pithiviers for 25 to 30 minutes, the smaller for about 20 minutes, until golden brown. Meanwhile, reduce the strained juices by a third, season with pepper and whisk in the butter to give a shiny jus. Serve the pithiviers with the jus.

LEMON SOLE *WITH* POINTED CABBAGE & A LEMON BUTTER SAUCE

SERVES FOUR

When visiting Copenhagen, should you suffer from a surfeit of new Nordic cuisine, may I recommend Claus Christensen's restaurant Gammel Mønt or Bo Jacobsen's restaurant opposite, Restaurationen? Both will give you what is essentially French cooking with a definite nod in the direction of Denmark. Claus's recipe was for a whole turbot cooked in a fabulously expensive turbot kettle. I hope he doesn't mind but I have taken the idea and used a lemon sole instead. I have written this as a sort of fish course somewhere between the starter and the main.

1 hispi (pointed cabbage)
150g unsalted butter, cubed
3 tsp salt
½ tsp sugar
1 lemon
5 rasps grated nutmeg
2 lemon soles,
    weighing about 300g,
    filleted and skinned
    (ask the fishmonger)
150ml milk
10 turns black peppermill
Small handful parsley,
    4 sprigs set aside, the
    rest roughly chopped

Remove the outer leaves of the cabbage. Cut it in half, remove the solid stalk and thinly slice the cabbage.

Melt 50g of the butter in a saucepan over medium heat, add 2 teaspoons of the salt, the sugar, the juice of half the lemon, the nutmeg and the sliced cabbage. Put a lid on the pan and cook for 5 to 10 minutes, stirring frequently at the beginning to ensure the cabbage doesn't catch.

Put the fillets side by side in a frying pan and add the milk, the pepper and 1 teaspoon of salt. Bring to the boil, turn the heat down low and cover. Poach for about 3 minutes. Remove the fillets from the pan and keep warm.

Pass the poaching liquor in the frying pan through a fine sieve and return to the pan. Bring to the boil and reduce the volume by half. Add the remaining cubes of butter (100g) and the juice of a quarter of the lemon and whisk until the butter has melted and the sauce has reduced down so that it is thick enough to coat the back of a spoon. Stir in the chopped parsley.

Put the cabbage on 4 warmed plates, place the fillets on top and pour the sauce over. Serve each plate with a sprig of parsley.

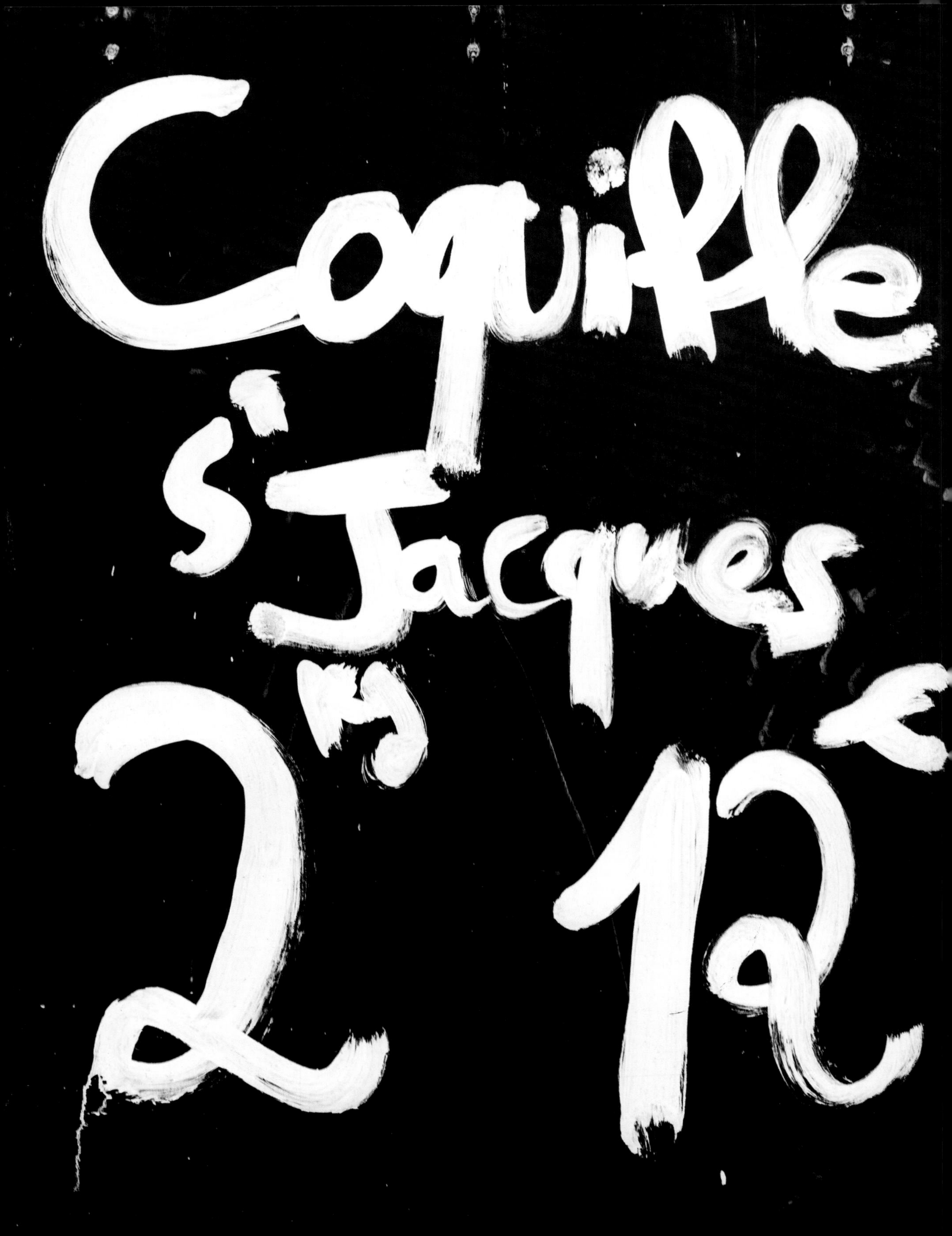

Coquille
S' Jacques
2^m 12

Coquille
S' Jacques
2^m 12

Coquille
S' Jacques
2ᵐ 12

CHEFFY SOLE À LA MEUNIÈRE

═ SERVES TWO ═

This recipe comes from the Grand Hotel in Bordeaux, and was prepared for me by the head chef Olivier Garnier. We filmed him cooking a whole Dover sole à la meunière. Though I have written recipes similar to his in the past, I have become a little more sympathetic to my readers over the years, in the sense that to cook a whole Dover sole you need a large, oval, Dover sole frying pan, which isn't cheap. So I have changed the recipe to fillets, but only for two people, because it is still quite a performance cooking this *à la minute* dish for any more at home. The accompaniments to this, the girolles and chestnuts, are a bit haute cuisine, but if you are feeling particularly amorous on a Saturday night then this is for you, maybe with a glass or two of nice white Bordeaux, such as Château Clos Floridène, to go with it.

2 x 200g Dover sole
    fillets, skinned
Salt and white pepper
30g plain flour
4 tbsp vegetable oil
60g unsalted butter
2 tbsp olive oil
60g girolles mushrooms
6 whole chestnuts, halved
2 tbsp *Beef stock* (page 307)
Zest ½ lemon
Handful flat-leaf parsley,
    chopped or chiffonade
½ lemon, cut into wedges

Season the fish with salt and white pepper and dust with the flour. Warm 2 tablespoons of the vegetable oil and a knob of the butter (25g) in a frying pan over medium-high heat. Fry the fish one at a time for 1½ minutes on each side, then keep warm.

Discard the frying oil and wipe the pan with kitchen paper. Add another knob of butter (25g) and cook until nutty and golden brown, then pour over the fish. Add the olive oil to the pan and sauté the girolles, then add the chestnuts, beef stock and lemon zest, along with the remaining 10g butter, and cook for a couple of minutes.

Serve each sole fillet with half of the mushroom and chestnut mixture poured over and around the fish, parsley sprinkled on top, and a lemon wedge on the side.

VIENNESE GULASCH WITH SPÄTZLE

=== SERVES SIX ===

I love gulasch. I learnt in Vienna that it is a simple dish. So often it comes with green and red peppers, tomatoes, mushrooms, even courgettes, when in fact it should be just good shin of beef, lots of onions – about three-quarters of the weight of the beef – sweet Hungarian paprika and caraway seeds. You can be permitted a small amount of tomato paste and some garlic, and that's about it. The only possible accompaniment is spätzle, tossed in butter and freshly grated nutmeg. This is a perfect dish for a large informal dinner on a Saturday night. *Recipe photograph overleaf*

100g lard
1.2kg onions, chopped
4 cloves garlic, grated
    or finely chopped
1 tbsp tomato paste
2 tbsp sweet paprika
1½ tbsp hot paprika
1 tsp caraway seeds, crushed
2 tsp cider vinegar
2 tsp brown sugar
1½ tsp salt
12 turns black peppermill
1 litre water
1.5kg shin of beef,
    cut into 3cm pieces

For the spätzle
500g plain flour
2 tsp salt, plus extra
    for cooking
4 eggs, beaten
250ml milk
80g butter
Few rasps nutmeg
8 turns black peppermill

Heat the lard in a large pot over medium heat and fry the onions until a deep golden brown, about 20 minutes.

Add the garlic, cook for 1 minute, then add the tomato paste, hot and sweet paprika, caraway seeds, vinegar, sugar, salt and pepper, and cover with the water. Bring to the boil, then add the beef, turn down the heat and simmer for 1¾–2 hours. Check fairly frequently and stir, adding more water to cover the meat if necessary.

For the spätzle, sift the flour and salt into a bowl. Add the eggs and, using a whisk, incorporate them into the flour. Still whisking, gradually add the milk until you have a thick batter. Cover and rest in the fridge for about 30 minutes.

Bring a large, deep pan of salted water to the boil, then turn down to a simmer. Rest a colander over the pan, ensuring it is not touching the water. Push the batter through the holes in the colander with a spatula. Cook for 2 to 3 minutes or until all the noodles have risen to the surface. Drain well.

Check the meat for tenderness. If not tender, add a little more water and cook for a little longer. If the sauce is too liquid, remove the meat and reduce over high heat.

Heat the butter in a frying pan until foaming. Add the spätzle and fry until golden and coated in the butter. Add the nutmeg and pepper, stir well and remove from the heat.

Serve the meat in the sauce with spätzle.

WIENER SCHNITZEL
WITH VIENNESE POTATO SALAD

=== SERVES FOUR ===

I feel a little smug being able to say I have witnessed the ultimate Wiener schnitzel being made. There are more definitive versions than you can shake a stick at, but since mine was at the Imperial Hotel in Vienna, cooked by the executive chef Rupert Schnait, I don't think you can deny my claim to authenticity. The three most important points, apart from the cut, which should be veal tenderloin, i.e. the strip loin without any fat, are: 1. It should be clarified butter and nothing but. 2. The breadcrumbs should be fine and dried out in the oven to a golden brown. 3. Cook in at least a centimetre of butter. The pan should be agitated to induce a slight soufflé effect on the flour, egg and breadcrumb coating. I would also argue that the must-have accompaniment is the potato salad, made with sunflower oil, onions, cider vinegar and a little beef stock.

600g veal tenderloin,
    cut on a slant into 4 slices
    about 1cm thick
Salt and freshly ground
    black pepper
50g plain flour
2 eggs, beaten
100g fine white *Breadcrumbs*
    (page 309)
200g *Clarified butter*
    (page 309)
1 lemon, cut into wedges

For the Viennese potato salad
600g new potatoes
175ml *Beef stock* (page 307)
1 small onion, very
    finely chopped
2 tbsp sunflower oil
2 tbsp cider vinegar
25g icing sugar
1 tsp salt
¼ tsp ground white pepper
Small bunch chives, chopped
2 radishes, cut into sticks

For the potato salad, boil the new potatoes in their skins until tender, 10 to 15 minutes. Allow to cool, then peel and slice thickly. Heat the beef stock. Dip in the cooked potatoes to 'glaze' them, then lift out with a slotted spoon and transfer to a salad bowl. Add the onion, oil, vinegar, sugar, salt and white pepper. Toss well, garnish with chives and radishes, and set aside.

Place the veal slices between sheets of clingfilm and beat, using a meat mallet or rolling pin, until about 3mm thick. Season with salt and pepper on both sides, then dip in flour, then egg, then breadcrumbs.

Heat the clarified butter in a large frying pan over high heat until a breadcrumb thrown in sizzles, then lower the schnitzels 2 at a time into the butter. Cook for about 3 minutes per side until the coating is a rich, deep, golden brown, agitating the pan a little to encourage the coating to soufflé up. Remove to a plate lined with kitchen paper to absorb the excess fat. Repeat with the remaining veal. Serve immediately with lemon wedges, and warm or cold potato salad.

ALMADRABA
SEARED TUNA WITH RED WINE, OLIVE OIL & AROMATIC HERBS

=== SERVES FOUR ===

A real joy of going to coastal Andalusia in May and June is that it is the season for bluefin tuna. They migrate from the Atlantic to the Mediterranean at this time and are caught in vast quantities just off Cadiz. There is global consternation about overfishing bluefin, but from what I can gather this particular fishery is well managed. This makes me feel happy because when it is as fresh as you get it in Cadiz, El Puerto de Santa Maria and Rota, to name but a few places, it is one of the best-tasting fish in the world. While I have always favoured eating my tuna rare, I also enjoy fish of this quality medium or well done. In this recipe a joint of tuna is marinated in red wine, then fried and roasted. The sauce made from a reduction of red wine and fish stock, finished with olive oil. It's sensational, and so is the chef, José Manuel Córdoba Serrano, in the restaurant where I had it, Ventorrillo el Chato, on the causeway that links Cadiz to the mainland.

400ml red wine
600g tuna, in one piece, about 4cm thick
90ml olive oil
100g carrot, finely chopped
100g onion, finely chopped
1 clove garlic, chopped
200ml *Fish stock* (page 307)
1 bay leaf
Small sprig thyme
Small sprig rosemary
½ tsp salt
6 turns black peppermill
Sauté potatoes (page 308), to serve

Boil the red wine for 1 minute to reduce the alcohol, then allow to cool and chill it. When cold, marinate the tuna steaks for 40 minutes. Remove the tuna and reserve the wine for the sauce.

Heat the oven to 200°C/gas 6.

Heat 1 tablespoon of the olive oil in a frying pan over high heat and sear the tuna steaks for about 1 minute each side. Set aside while you prepare the sauce.

In the same pan, heat the remaining olive oil over medium heat. Add the carrot, onion and garlic and sweat for about 10 minutes. Increase the heat, add the reserved red wine, almost all of the fish stock, herbs, salt and pepper, and cook for 10 to 12 minutes to reduce by two-thirds.

Transfer the vegetables and sauce to an ovenproof dish, and place the tuna on top. Cook for about 8 to 12 minutes for pink-centred tuna. If you like your tuna more done, cook for 12 to 15 minutes.

Remove from the oven and slice the tuna about 1cm to 1.5cm thick. If necessary, reduce down the juices, or, if already too reduced, add the remaining fish stock. Use to coat part of the fish and serve with sauté potatoes.

URTA A LA ROTEÑA
BAKED SEA BREAM ROTA-STYLE
═ SERVES TWO ═

This dish originally comes from Rota in the Bay of Cadiz, but it is popular
throughout the area. Traditionally made with the large, local, red-banded bream,
I have adapted it for gilt-head bream, which you can get easily in the UK. It is a farmed
fish, but none the worse for it. They don't come much bigger than 400g so I suggest
cooking two individual fish to serve two people. If you are lucky enough to get hold of a
1.4kg or 1.5kg fish, double the quantities of the other ingredients and you can serve four.
Pre-cooking the vegetables in the oven allows for a briefer cooking time for the fish.

Recipe photograph overleaf

3 large waxy potatoes, peeled
Salt and freshly ground
 black pepper
5 tbsp olive oil
1 large onion, sliced
1 clove garlic, chopped
1 large green pepper,
 seeded and sliced
300g tomatoes, skinned
 and chopped
1 bay leaf
2 x 400g whole sea bream,
 scaled and gutted
60ml water
Juice ½ lemon
6 black peppercorns
60ml dry sherry
Small handful flat-leaf
 parsley, leaves chopped

For the picada
Small handful flat-leaf
 parsley, chopped
2 large cloves garlic,
 roughly chopped
½ tsp sea salt

Heat the oven to 180°C/gas 4.

Cut the potatoes into thick slices. Arrange on an ovenproof
dish large enough to accommodate the sea bream later.
Season with salt and pepper and drizzle with 2 tablespoons
of the olive oil. Bake in the oven for about 20 minutes.

In a frying pan, warm 2 tablespoons of the olive oil over
medium-low heat. Fry the onion, garlic and green pepper
until soft, 10 to 15 minutes. Add the tomatoes, bay leaf and
a little water, cover with a lid and continue cooking for about
15 minutes.

Season the fish with ½ teaspoon salt and 10 turns of the
black peppermill and place on top of the cooked potato slices.

Make the picada using a mortar and pestle: grind the
parsley, garlic and sea salt together, then spread it over the
fish. Add the water and lemon juice to the dish, then pour
the tomato mixture over everything.

Drizzle over the remaining tablespoon of olive oil, add the
black peppercorns and sherry and transfer to the oven to bake
for 20 to 25 minutes. Scatter the parsley over the top and
serve immediately.

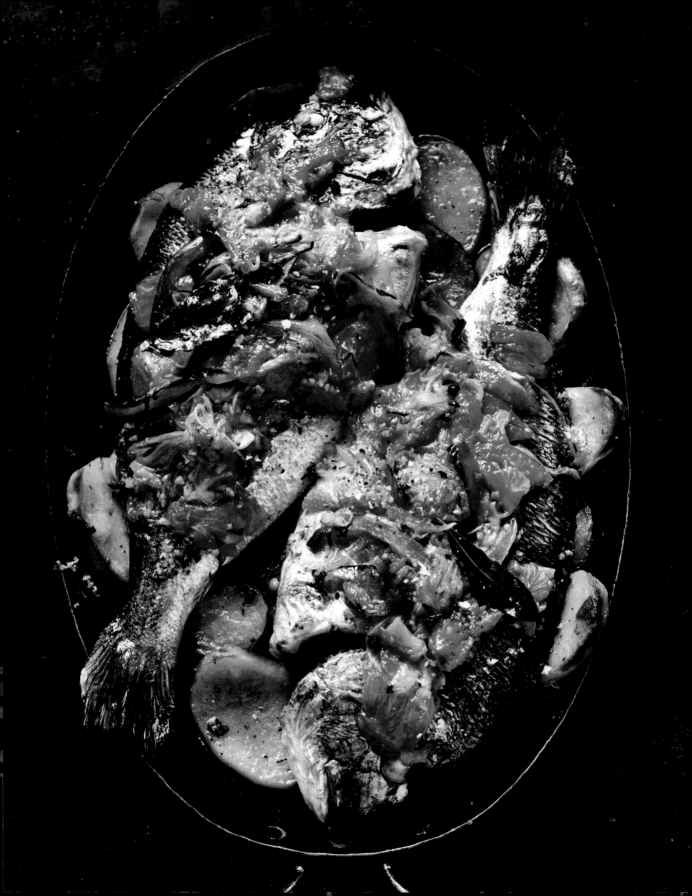

KÖNIGSBERGER KLOPSE
VEAL & PORK DUMPLINGS
WITH BEETROOT & TABASCO
=== SERVES FOUR ===

Of all the restaurants I went to in Berlin, La Soupe Populaire is the most memorable, not just for the cooking, but also the location in the old Bötzow brewery in the former East. They last made beer in 1949, but the old equipment is still there. Chef Michael Jaeger cooks traditional food in a modern way. This is a veal dumpling, but light as a feather, with an exquisite sauce of chicken stock, cream and white wine. The crowning glory is the beetroot salad, flavoured startlingly with Tabasco. It might sound as weird as the art but it works a treat.

500g minced veal
500g minced pork
1 tbsp capers, roughly chopped
1 tbsp parsley, chopped
125g dried white *Breadcrumbs*
   (page 309)
2 eggs, lightly beaten
1 tsp salt
20 turns white peppermill
2 tbsp sweet German mustard
   (*süßer Senf*)
1 litre *Chicken stock* (page 307)
30g butter

For the mashed potato
1kg potato
75g butter
50ml single cream
Salt and freshly ground
   black pepper
Freshly grated nutmeg

For the sauce
150ml double cream
125g butter
4 tbsp fine semolina
60ml sweet white wine

For the apple and beetroot salad
225ml cloudy apple juice
½ tsp Tabasco
2 tbsp cider vinegar
2 small cooked beetroot, grated
2 small Cox's apples, peeled
   and grated

For the apple and beetroot salad, bring the apple juice, Tabasco and cider vinegar to the boil in a pan and reduce right down to a syrupy 2 tablespoons. Allow to cool, then pour over the grated apple and beetroot and marinate for a couple of hours in the fridge.

In a large bowl combine the minced veal and pork with the capers, parsley and 100g breadcrumbs. Add the eggs and season with salt, white pepper and mustard and mix everything together well. With wet hands form the mixture into 8 roughly equal-size balls.

Warm the stock in a pan over medium heat. Add the meatballs and simmer for 20 minutes.

In a frying pan, melt the butter and fry the remaining 25g breadcrumbs until golden. Set aside.

Meanwhile, boil the potatoes until tender, then drain and mash with the butter and cream and season to taste with salt, pepper and nutmeg.

For the sauce, ladle off 450ml of the chicken stock and strain it into a separate pan over medium heat. Whisk in the cream, then add the butter and keep whisking until the butter melts. Add the semolina and keep whisking for about 5 minutes until the sauce thickens. Add the sweet wine and simmer for about 2 minutes, then take off the heat.

Serve 2 lozenges of the mashed potato shaped with 2 dessertspoons along with 2 of the meatballs for each person. Top with a sprinkling of fried breadcrumbs, place a spoonful of the salad alongside and spoon some of the sauce around the plate.

DUCK RAGÙ *with* TAGLIATELLE

═ SERVES SIX TO EIGHT ═

Duck ragù is exactly the sort of rustic Italian dish I love. It was made for me in Bologna from a roast duck; the chef took the meat off the bone, chopped it and added it to onions, garlic, carrots and celery, tomato paste and wine. This goes perfectly with home-made tagliatelle and lots of Parmesan, of course. Interestingly, there is a complicated formula for the ideal width of tagliatelle, based on the ratio of height to width of the largest remaining tower in Bologna, the Asinelli. Suffice to say that it should be around 6.5 to 7mm wide when raw. *Recipe photograph overleaf*

For the duck
1.8kg Gressingham duck
2 tsp salt
3 tbsp olive oil
1 onion, chopped
2 cloves garlic, chopped
2 large carrots, chopped
2 sticks celery, chopped
2 tbsp tomato paste
150ml red wine
1 tsp salt
12 turns black peppermill
½ tsp sugar
250ml *Duck stock* (see below)
Small handful flat-leaf
    parsley, chopped

For the duck stock
The duck carcass, plus neck
    and giblets if available
2 carrots, unpeeled,
    roughly chopped
1 large onion,
    roughly chopped
2 sticks celery,
    roughly chopped
1 tsp salt
½ tsp black peppercorns
1 sprig thyme

For the pasta
600g 00 pasta flour,
    plus extra for dusting
½ tsp salt
6 eggs, beaten

Heat the oven to 190°C/gas 5.

Prepare the duck by pricking the skin all over and rubbing in 1 teaspoon of the salt. Place the duck on a trivet in a roasting tin and roast for 1 hour 45 minutes. Collect any fat in a jam jar for roasting potatoes at a later date. Cool the duck and strip the meat off the carcass, chopping it a little.

Make the stock. Put the duck carcass, neck and giblets in a large pan and cover with water. Add the carrot, onion, celery, salt, peppercorns and thyme, bring to a boil, then turn down to a simmer and cook for 3 to 4 hours. Strain before use.

Make the pasta by combining the flour, salt and eggs in a food processor to 'breadcrumb' stage, then tip out on to a lightly floured board and knead for 3 to 4 minutes until smooth and elastic. Form into a ball, wrap in clingfilm and allow to rest for at least 30 minutes before rolling.

Roll the pasta dough out to 2mm thick, then run through the wide cutters on a pasta machine or cut into tagliatelle ribbons by hand. Set aside to dry until ready to cook.

Heat the olive oil in a large pan over medium heat and sweat the onions, garlic, carrot and celery until soft, about 10 minutes. Add the tomato paste and red wine, the remaining salt, pepper and sugar, then increase the heat and reduce by half. Add 250ml of the duck stock and reduce down to a thick sauce. Add the shredded duck meat to the pan and heat through for 10 to 15 minutes with a lid on the pan.

Boil the fresh pasta for about 3 to 4 minutes in plenty of salted water. Drain well, then add to the pan with the ragù, stir in the parsley and serve in warmed bowls.

PORK BELLY SLICES WITH PARSLEY SAUCE & LOVAGE POTATOES

SERVES FOUR

This recipe comes from the Red Cottage at Klampenborg just outside Copenhagen. We went there to join Anita Klemensen and Lars Thomsen for an afternoon's foraging on the seashore and in the woods, followed by a cookery session with Anita in her kitchen. The restaurant is like something out of a fairytale: a cottage in the woods painted red, with the sea beyond. We picked white nettle flowers, dog rose petals, sea purslane and onion cress from the beach and wood sorrel and ramson berries in the woods. Like many other new Nordic chefs with a good reputation, all her dishes were made with ingredients from within ten miles of the restaurant. Much as I liked her food, as is so often the case it's just not something someone could cook at home. You need masses of storage space, plenty of worktop and a pile of tweezers. So it was with some relief, wanting to bring a recipe back from a very cheerful and convivial afternoon, that I noted that Anita and Lars had prepared what is possibly the Danish national dish for the staff and the film crew. We ate it with gusto.

800g new potatoes,
    peeled and kept whole
½ tsp salt
Large sprig fresh lovage
1 tsp lard or goose fat
8 slices belly pork, about
    1cm thick (about 1kg)
25g butter
25g plain flour
300ml full-fat milk
½ tsp salt
10 turns black peppermill
50g flat-leaf parsley,
    leaves finely chopped

Boil the potatoes in plenty of water with the salt and the lovage until tender. Drain and reserve 150ml of the cooking water. Discard the lovage.

Melt the lard in a large heavy frying pan over medium-high heat and fry the pork for 8 to 10 minutes on each side, then take off the heat.

Melt the butter in a saucepan over a medium heat, add the flour and stir to make a roux. Cook for 1 to 2 minutes, then gradually add the milk, stirring all the time until smooth. Add the reserved potato water. Taste and season with the salt and pepper. Add the parsley, stir through and cook for 1 minute.

Serve the pork and potatoes with the parsley sauce.

SICILIAN FRITELLA RISOTTO

SERVES FOUR

I rang my assistant Portia Spooner while I was in Palermo in the spring, all enthusiastic about the beautiful small artichokes and fresh beans and peas in the markets. I asked her to find a recipe for a risotto with these three ingredients in it. She wrote back to say she couldn't find one but had come up with her own. This is it, and completely delightful too. If you're lucky enough to find really tender artichokes, simply cut about ten of them in half – you won't need to trim them. *Recipe photograph overleaf*

3 globe artichokes
Juice 1 lemon or 1 tbsp
   white wine vinegar
1–1.2 litres *Vegetable stock*
   (page 307)
40g butter
3 tbsp olive oil
1 onion, chopped
1 clove garlic, chopped
   or grated
300g Arborio or carnaroli rice
125ml dry white wine
200g fresh broad beans,
   double podded if not young
   (600–700g weight in pods)
200g fresh peas (about 600g
   weight in pods)
Zest and juice ½ small lemon
½–1 tsp salt
8 turns black peppermill
70g pecorino, freshly grated

Prepare the globe artichokes. Remove the stem to within 1cm of the base. Peel off the outer leaves until you reach the pale-coloured centre. Remove the hairy choke with a teaspoon. Pare off any remaining outer leaves with a sharp knife. Cut into 6 wedges and plunge into a bowl of cold water to which you've added the lemon juice or vinegar to prevent it discolouring.

Heat the stock in a saucepan. Melt the half the butter with the olive oil in a wide pan over medium-low heat and sweat the onion and garlic for 5 to 10 minutes until soft. Add the rice and stir well to coat the grains. Add the white wine and stir until it has been absorbed by the rice, then start adding the vegetable stock a ladleful at a time, stirring until it is absorbed, which will take about 20 minutes.

After about 12 minutes, in a separate pan, cook the artichoke wedges in boiling water for 5 to 7 minutes until tender. Remove from the water and set aside. Add the broad beans and peas and boil for about 3 minutes, then drain. Add the cooked vegetables to the risotto and heat through.

Remove from the heat and stir through the lemon zest and juice, the remaining butter, salt to taste, pepper and half the pecorino cheese. Serve immediately with the rest of the pecorino cheese.

PETZ'S SPICY CABBAGE
WITH SMOKED HAM

=== SERVES FOUR TO SIX AS A SIDE DISH ===

Christian Petz is a highly regarded, Michelin-starred chef in Vienna who has turned his back on 'fine dining' and concentrated on really gutsy Viennese cooking, often using types of offal that most people wouldn't be able to buy, let alone cook, such as heart and lungs. He cooked a dish called *Grammelknödel* for me, a dumpling made with crisp pork rind; you can find the recipe on my website rickstein.com. However, the cabbage dish that accompanied the dumplings was exceptional, and I had to have it in the book. I certainly wouldn't have wanted to miss including a recipe from a man I have enormous respect for. What I loved about it were the flavours of speck, caraway, chilli and red peppers with the cabbage.

1 tsp lard
2 slices speck or prosciutto
   or smoked Austrian
   ham, chopped
1 onion, finely chopped
1 clove garlic, sliced
½ white cabbage
   (about 400–450g),
   finely shredded
½ tsp salt
½ tsp ground caraway seeds
¼ red pepper, finely chopped
1 pickled chilli, chopped
50ml white wine

Warm the lard in a frying pan over medium heat, and fry the speck (or its alternative) until it starts to brown, about 3 minutes. Add the onion and garlic and sauté for 2 to 3 minutes, then add the shredded white cabbage, season with the salt and caraway and cook for 2 minutes. Finally add the red pepper, pickled chilli and white wine, and cook for 3 to 5 minutes. Serve at once.

SATURDAY NIGHT DESSERTS

It's generally true to say, however magnificent the main course of your Saturday dinner is – grilled lobster, turbot, ribs of beef roasted or grilled, meat aged for days in Himalayan salt-encrusted cold rooms – the most talked-about part of the meal will still be the dessert, certainly if my wife's enthusiasm for puddings is anything to go by. There's a charming paragraph in Brillat-Savarin's book on gastronomy, *The Physiology of Taste*: 'I was sitting one day at a great entertainment, and saw opposite to me a very pretty woman with a very sensual face. I leaned towards my neighbour and said, that the lady with such features must be gourmande . . . The beginning was not favourable . . . During the first two courses, the young woman ate with a discretion which really amazed me. The dessert came, it was brilliant as it was abundant, and gave me some hopes. I was not deceived, for she not only ate what was set before her, but sent for dishes which were at the other end of the table. She tasted everything, and we were surprised that so small a stomach could contain so much. My diagnostics succeeded and science triumphed.'

Dessert should not be an afterthought. You need to build up to it. If I'm cooking dinner for any more than two people on a Saturday night, there's got to be a good long pause after the main course before the pudding comes because this is the time when conversation becomes intense. Food is then just a distraction from topics such as the affair of one of your friends, how overweight another has become, Boris Johnson, the aggression of cyclists, the non-existent British summer, or how beautiful Cornwall is although it's being ruined by everyone going there.

When the pudding does arrive after this essential gap, it's suddenly very welcome. You can, of course, bring out the cheese at this stage, as the French do, but it doesn't work for me. A good, honest, freshly cooked pudding is exactly the right thing. Or, if you've let go a bit with the alcohol and you predicted that might happen, something you prepared earlier will be a godsend.

In the first category I recommend Kaiserschmarrn on page 226: buttery souffléd pancakes with a plum compote, essential to make at the last minute; in the latter category Apple Strudel (page 224), Smashed Liquorice Meringues with Berries and Chocolate Cream (page 240), or the ultra-simple Lemon Fromage from Copenhagen on page 234: all will provoke exclamations of joy.

TARTE DE AMÊNDOA
ALMOND TART
⸺ SERVES EIGHT ⸺

This tart is unusual in that it is simply butterscotch-tasting almonds baked in a pastry case. There is no almond paste (frangipani) filling, which makes it light, crisp and crunchy. It's lovely as it is but you can also dot it with fresh raspberries and sprinkle with icing sugar for something a bit more flash.

For the pastry
150g plain flour, sifted,
    plus extra for dusting
75g butter
60g caster sugar
1 egg yolk
2 tsp cold water

For the filling
225g flaked almonds
120g butter
120g caster sugar
4 tbsp milk

You need a loose-bottomed, 24cm fluted tart tin. Make the pastry in a food processor. Mix the flour, butter and sugar to breadcrumb stage, then add the egg yolk and water and mix until the dough comes together. Roll out on a floured worktop to 5mm thick, a little bit bigger than the base of the tin.

Line the tin, then use your fingers to press the pastry into the corners and about 1cm up the sides to create a small lip around the edge. Cover with clingfilm and leave in the fridge for at least 30 minutes.

Heat the oven to 190°C/gas 5.

Remove the clingfilm and prick the pastry base all over lightly with a fork. Line with greaseproof paper and baking beans or lentils, and bake for 15 minutes. Remove the baking beans and paper and return to the oven for 3 to 4 minutes to dry out the base without colouring.

Make the filling. Toast the flaked almonds in a dry frying pan over medium-high heat for 2 to 3 minutes until a light golden brown, keeping a close eye on them. Tip into a bowl.

Put the butter, sugar and milk in the frying pan over medium heat. When the sugar has dissolved and the butter melted, bring up to a boil and boil for 1 minute. Add the toasted almond slivers and mix well before turning into the pastry case.

Bake for 15 to 20 minutes until a rich golden brown. Remove from the oven and allow to cool before serving. Serve warm or cold.

AQUITAINE FLOURLESS CHOCOLATE CAKE

≡ SERVES EIGHT ≡

There is something about the mousse-like texture of this baked flourless chocolate cake which makes it seem like a restaurant dessert, the sort of thing you would serve with raspberries or cherries, crème fraîche and a dusting of cocoa.

285g dark chocolate
140g unsalted butter
5 large eggs, separated
140g caster sugar
Cocoa powder, for dusting

To serve
Crème fraîche, raspberries
  or cherries

Heat the oven to 160°C/gas 3. Grease a 23cm springform tin and line the base.

Break up the chocolate, place in a bowl with the butter and melt over a pan of barely simmering water. When melted, set aside.

In a separate bowl, whisk the egg yolks and 100g of the caster sugar until pale and creamy. Stir into the melted chocolate.

In a third bowl, whisk the egg whites to very soft peaks, then whisk in the remaining 40g sugar, as if making meringue. Mix one spoonful of the egg white into the chocolate mixture to loosen it, then carefully fold in the remaining egg white, leaving no pockets of white in the mixture.

Carefully pour into the cake tin and bake for 30 to 35 minutes, or until a skewer comes out clean. Leave to cool a little in the tin, then dust with cocoa powder. Serve slightly warm or cold, with berries or cherries and crème fraîche.

CINNAMON CHURROS
WITH SPICED CHOCOLATE SAUCE

≡ SERVES FOUR ≡

Cadiz is reputed to have the best churros in Andalusia. I actually found those at a seafood place, called Cervecería Bajamar, where you can order a cup of cinnamon-flavoured chocolate with freshly fried churros to dip, as well as the obligatory *café con leche*.

1.5 litres sunflower oil,
    for deep-frying
100g plain flour
150ml full-fat milk
150ml water
2 eggs, beaten
50g golden caster sugar
½ tsp ground cinnamon

For the dipping sauce
100ml double cream
75ml full-fat milk
6cm cinnamon stick
2 tsp fennel seeds
Pinch chilli flakes
1 star anise
100g dark chocolate
    (72 per cent cocoa solids)
1 tbsp golden caster sugar
Pinch salt

Make the chocolate dipping sauce. Scald the cream, milk and spices in a saucepan – heat to just before boiling point – then take off the heat and allow to infuse for about 20 minutes.

Break the chocolate into pieces and put into a bowl. Strain the milk and cream and return to a clean pan with the caster sugar and salt, bring back up to a scald and pour over the chocolate. Stir until melted. If too thick, add a little more milk to let the mixture down. Set aside while you make the churros.

Heat the oil in a heavy-based pan to a temperature of 190°C, using a probe or sugar thermometer to check. Heat the oven to 150°C/gas 2.

Sift the flour on to a sheet of greaseproof paper and set aside. Bring the milk and water to the boil in pan, take the pan off the heat and, using the greaseproof paper as a chute, add the flour all at once. Stir vigorously until you have a smooth paste. Leave to cool slightly, then add the beaten eggs a little at a time until you have a smooth and silky batter that reluctantly drops off a wooden spoon.

Line a plate with kitchen paper and place alongside the hob. Fit a piping bag with a large star nozzle and spoon the batter into the piping bag. Hold the bag over the hot oil and carefully squeeze in a few 15cm lengths of the batter. Leave to fry for 4 minutes, turning them after 2 minutes. Remove with a slotted spoon to the lined plate to drain, then transfer to the oven to keep warm while you cook the rest.

Toss the warm churros in the mixed caster sugar and cinnamon and serve with the spiced chocolate dip. Any remaining dip can be turned into a delicious hot chocolate by adding hot milk.

APPLE STRUDEL

SERVES FOUR TO SIX

My recipe is light on breadcrumbs and heavy on apple. I find a lot of strudels can be stodgy. A small amount of breadcrumb in the filling is essential but so is a lightness and tartness, which could otherwise be lost. You can serve this with custard, or with Chantilly cream, which is cream whipped with caster sugar. Mind you, after many a skiing holiday I am rather a fan of cream foam from an aerosol tin, which Florence, the daughter of Portia Spooner, my assistant, refers to as squirty cream.

750g Bramley apples, peeled, cored, quartered and sliced
1½ tsp ground cinnamon
Zest ½ lemon
2 tsp lemon juice
100g golden caster sugar
75g raisins
95g butter
40g dried white *Breadcrumbs* (page 309)
6 large sheets filo pastry
1 tbsp icing sugar, for dusting
Cream, ice cream or custard, to serve

Mix the apples with the cinnamon, lemon zest and juice, caster sugar and raisins. In a small frying pan, melt 20g of the butter and fry the breadcrumbs until golden, then add to the apple mixture.

Heat the oven to 190°C/gas 5. Line a baking sheet with baking parchment.

Melt the rest of the butter (75g) in a pan. Place a clean tea towel on the worktop with the long edge towards you. Place a sheet of the filo on top, and brush with some of the melted butter. Lay another sheet on top, and repeat until you have used all the filo. Now pile the filling on the filo, leaving about 3cm clear all round. Tuck the ends in, then, using the tea towel to help, roll the pastry away from you to enclose all the filling. Transfer the roll seam-side down to the lined baking sheet and brush with the rest of the melted butter. Bake for 40 to 45 minutes until golden.

Allow to cool to room temperature and dust with icing sugar. Slice and serve with cream, ice cream or custard.

BUTTERY SOUFFLÉD PANCAKES
WITH PLUM COMPOTE

SERVES FOUR

Kaiserschmarrn is shredded pancake fried in butter with sugar; it's Kaiser Franz Joseph's 'little bit of nonsense'. He loved this dish. It's just as gorgeous as our trifle or a good Eton mess. Essential to make it and serve it straight away.

2 eggs
125g plain flour, sifted
120ml milk
½ tsp bicarbonate of soda
30g vanilla sugar
    or caster sugar and
    ½ tsp vanilla extract
Pinch salt
100ml double or whipping
    cream, whipped
50g butter
50g raisins, soaked
    in 3 tbsp warm rum
30g caster sugar
20g icing sugar, for dusting

For the plum compote
180ml water
90g caster sugar
1 cinnamon stick
400g plums, halved
    and stones removed

To make the compote, heat the water and sugar in saucepan over medium heat. When the sugar has dissolved, raise the heat, bring to the boil and cook for 1 minute, then turn down to a simmer. Add the cinnamon stick and plums. Cover and cook gently for about 5 to 10 minutes, until the plums are soft but not mushy – this will depend on how ripe the plums are. Remove from the heat and set aside.

Whisk the eggs in a mixing bowl. Add the flour and milk, continuing to whisk. Add the bicarbonate of soda, vanilla sugar (or caster sugar and vanilla extract) and salt. Fold in the whipped cream.

Melt the butter in a non-stick frying pan over medium heat and pour in the batter. Add the soaked raisins to the pan on top of the batter. When the pancake holds its shape but is still soft and moist in the centre, after 3 to 4 minutes, cut it into pieces in the pan using a wooden spatula. Sprinkle with caster sugar, flip over, and continue to cook and flip over until the pieces are nicely caramelized all over, about a further 3 to 4 minutes. Serve sprinkled liberally with icing sugar and with warm or cold plum compote on the side.

TOCINILLO DE CIELO
A FLOURLESS FLAN

In Spain virtually any restaurant you go into will serve *flan*, a firm custard made from eggs, flour and milk, finished with a caramel coating. What makes this Andalusian version different is that it is made without milk or flour, so it's very light. It is a little on the sweet side, which is why I have made the servings quite small. The perfect accompaniment to an espresso, or serve them with segments of fresh orange.
Recipe photograph overleaf

For the caramel
200g granulated sugar
2 tbsp water

For the custard
400g white caster sugar
500ml water
12 egg yolks

Heat the oven to 160°C/gas 3. Place 6 ramekins or individual aluminium pudding moulds in a deep roasting tin in the oven to warm while you make the caramel.

Put the sugar and water for the caramel into a saucepan. Dissolve the sugar slowly over a low heat, stirring with a wooden spoon. When fully dissolved, stop stirring, and boil until the sugar turns a dark amber colour, 5 to 10 minutes. Keep watching as it can burn quickly. Remove from the heat and divide the caramel between the warmed ramekins or moulds.

For the custard, in a fresh saucepan dissolve the caster sugar in the water and, when fully dissolved, turn up the heat and boil rapidly until the syrup reaches thread stage, 110°C on a sugar thermometer or probe. Set aside to cool.

Put the egg yolks in a bowl and mix with a wooden spoon. Gradually beat in the cooled sugar syrup – you do not want to incorporate lots of air. Divide this custard between the caramel-lined ramekins. It won't fill them.

Pour boiling water into the roasting tin to create a bain-marie. Cover with foil to keep the steam inside and cook the custards until set: 40 minutes in metal moulds or 50 minutes in ramekins. Remove from the bain-marie and allow to cool, then transfer to the fridge for at least 2 hours before serving. To serve, run a sharp knife round the edge of the mould to loosen the custard, then dip in a bowl of boiling water to release the caramel. Invert on to plates or dishes and serve.

LA TUPINA CRUSHADES
WITH CEPS & GRAPES

=== SERVES SIX ===

Even though I was visiting Bordeaux at the heart of the mushroom season, it was still surprising to find ceps on the menu as part of a dessert. I had to try it and was agreeably surprised. The mushrooms are fried in butter, then sprinkled in sugar, slightly caramelized and served warm.

100g plain flour, sifted
200g polenta
110g caster sugar
Pinch salt
1 litre full-fat milk
1 vanilla pod, split,
    or 1 tsp vanilla extract
1 tsp orange blossom water
Vegetable oil, for greasing
40g butter
300g cep/porcini
    mushrooms, sliced
100g green seedless
    grapes, whole
1 tbsp icing sugar,
    for dusting

Combine the flour, polenta, 50g of the sugar and the salt in a saucepan. Pour the milk into a jug. Scrape the vanilla seeds into the milk or add the extract, and add the orange blossom water. Using a whisk, gradually add the milk to the dry ingredients, ensuring that no lumps form.

When you have a smooth paste, put the pan on the heat, bring the mixture up to the boil and stir continuously for 2 to 3 minutes. Turn the heat down to very low and keep stirring for about 20 minutes until you have a thick paste. When you draw a wooden spoon through, it should leave a clear parting. Remove from the heat and spread in a thin, even layer on a lightly oiled board or baking tray. An oiled palette knife will help achieve a smooth result. Set aside to cool and solidify.

When the mixture is stiff enough, use an 8cm pastry cutter to stamp out 12 circles or a knife to cut out 12 squares or diamonds.

Melt the half the butter in a frying pan over medium heat and fry the dough until golden, about 3 to 4 minutes on each side.

Meanwhile, in a separate pan over high heat, fry the mushrooms in the rest of the butter for 3 to 4 minutes. Sprinkle over the remaining 60g sugar and the grapes, and continue cooking until the mushrooms are slightly caramelized and the grapes are warmed through, about 3 to 4 minutes. Serve the warm crushades dusted with icing sugar with the warm fried ceps and grapes.

PANNA COTTA WITH SALTED PISTACHIO CREAM

═ SERVES EIGHT ═

This is an ideal recipe for a dinner party. It can all be made in advance, it looks smart and the pistachio brittle is irresistible. You'll hear people say, 'Oh my God, this is amazing,' to which I say, 'That's Bologna for you!' The pistachio brittle makes more than you need so keep the rest to sprinkle on ice creams or cakes.

For the panna cotta
4 x 2g leaves gelatine
700ml double cream
200ml full-fat milk
1 vanilla pod
225g caster sugar

For the salted pistachio cream
130g shelled pistachios
30g butter, plus extra
    for greasing
¼ tsp sea salt flakes
80g caster sugar
3 tbsp water
300ml double cream

Soak the gelatine leaves in a bowl of cold water for 5 minutes. In a large pan over medium-low heat, warm the cream and milk with the vanilla pod and sugar and stir until the sugar has dissolved. Increase the heat, bring up to a simmer, then remove from the heat. Take out the vanilla pod, split and scrape the seeds back into the cream and milk mixture. Drain the gelatine leaves, squeeze out any excess water and stir into the mixture until dissolved. Divide between 8 small glasses or coffee cups. Cool completely then chill for at least 4 hours or overnight.

For the salted pistachio cream, toast 100g of the pistachio nuts in a dry pan over medium heat for 1 to 2 minutes, shaking the pan constantly so the nuts do not catch and burn. Roughly chop the toasted nuts. Butter a shallow metal baking tray well and scatter the toasted pistachios and sea salt over it.

Put the caster sugar, 30g butter and water into a heavy-based pan over medium heat and heat gently to dissolve the sugar. Increase the heat and boil for about 5 minutes or until the mixture turns a deep golden brown. Working fast, pour the caramel over the nuts on the tray. Set aside to cool and harden.

When hard, break up with a rolling pin and blitz in a processor into a very coarse 'powder'. Fold about 80g of the pistachio brittle powder into the double cream, and keep the rest for serving.

Roughly chop the remaining, untoasted nuts.

When ready to serve, run a sharp knife around the edge of each glass. Dip each one into a bowl of boiling water for about 10 seconds to loosen the mixture, then turn out on to serving plates. Spoon a pool of pistachio cream around each panna cotta and sprinkle over the roughly chopped nuts and a little more of the pistachio brittle.

LEMON FROMAGE

=== SERVES SIX ===

I first met Paul Cunningham in Sydney about six years ago. I had become quite familiar with Noma by then. He told me he had turned down the opportunity to be head chef there because being British it didn't seem correct to be the leading light in new Nordic cuisine. However, his heart is very much with the movement, even though he's not averse to pointing out some of its absurdities. I don't want any more wood sorrel in my life, he says. He now has a restaurant in Jutland called Henne Kirkeby Kro. I am very keen to go there because I know it'll be great cooking. We had a little picnic on the water in Copenhagen and he brought new potatoes cooked with lovage, fat white asparagus with a smoked cheese dip, small local brown shrimps with lemon mayonnaise and dill and spiced herrings from Christiansø, but just as we were leaving, almost as an afterthought, he and his sous chef Jesper Krabbe gave us a large bowl of this to eat. It was gone in seconds, it was that good. You really do need organic, unsprayed lemons for this.

3 eggs, separated
100g caster sugar
3 x 2g leaves gelatine
Zest and juice 3 small lemons
300ml whipping cream

Using an electric beater, whisk the yolks and sugar until smooth, light and creamy, making sure the sugar has completely dissolved.

Soak the gelatine leaves in cold water for 5 minutes. Squeeze out any excess water, then put the leaves in a small pan with 2 tablespoons of the lemon juice. Dissolve over a low heat – this will take a matter of seconds. Remove quickly from the heat. Stir in the remaining lemon juice and the lemon zest.

Whip 250ml of the cream to soft peaks. Fold in the gelatine and lemon mixture. Fold the cream and lemon mixture into the egg yolks and sugar.

Whisk the egg whites to soft peaks. Fold the egg whites into the lemon mixture and incorporate well, being careful not to knock out all the air.

Pour into a serving bowl and chill well for 3 to 4 hours. Just before serving, whip the remaining cream and pipe or spoon on to the top of the dish.

PISTACHIO GELATO IN BRIOCHE BUNS

═ SERVES SIX TO EIGHT ═

Sicily is famous for its pistachios, particularly those grown on the slopes of Etna.
A fabulous mid-morning treat in Palermo is freshly baked brioche and pistachio
ice cream. An unlikely combination but, trust me, a truly wonderful one. I made
my ice cream quite grainy with freshly blitzed pistachios and not a whiff of
that ghastly pistachio flavour you get in many ice creams.

100g unsalted shelled
  pistachios, plus extra,
  chopped, to serve
500ml full-fat milk
5 large egg yolks
150g caster sugar
¼–½ tsp green food colouring
  (depending on strength)

For the brioche buns
275g strong white flour,
  plus extra for dusting
30g caster sugar
1 tsp salt
1 tsp (5g) instant dried yeast
70ml warm full-fat milk
3 eggs, beaten, plus 1 egg,
  for glaze
100g unsalted butter,
  softened
Vegetable oil, for greasing

For the buns, use a food mixer fitted with a dough hook. Put
the flour, sugar and salt in the mixer bowl. Add the yeast, milk,
3 eggs and soft butter and mix on a slow speed for 2 minutes,
then increase the speed and mix for 5 minutes until the dough
is soft and elastic. It will be quite sticky. With a spatula, scrape
into a well-oiled bowl and cover the bowl with clingfilm.
Refrigerate for at least 6 hours or overnight, which will make
the dough much easier to handle.

Take the dough from the fridge, divide it into 6 to 8 pieces
and shape into rolls on a lightly floured board. Line a couple
of baking sheets with baking parchment. Arrange the buns
on the sheets and leave to rise for about 2 hours.

Heat the oven to 180°C/gas 4.

Glaze the buns with the beaten egg and bake for 17 to
20 minutes until risen and a deep golden brown. Cool on
a wire rack.

Toast the 100g pistachios in a dry frying pan for 1 to 2
minutes. Allow to cool, then finely chop in a food processor.

Combine the pistachio crumbs with the milk in a saucepan.
Bring up to the boil and turn off the heat.

In a large bowl whisk the egg yolks with the sugar, ideally
with a hand-held whisk, until creamy, about 3 minutes. Gradually
whisk in the milk mixture. Return this custard to the saucepan.
Stir over low-medium heat until it thickens slightly and coats
the back of spoon, which will take 6 to 10 minutes. Do not
allow the mixture to boil or the eggs will scramble.

Draw off the heat and stir in the food colouring. Refrigerate
the custard until cold, then churn in an ice-cream machine.
Transfer to a plastic box with a lid and freeze until ready
to serve.

Remove from the freezer 5 minutes before serving to
soften slightly. Serve in brioche rolls sprinkled with a few
extra chopped pistachios.

MERINGUE *AND* ZABAGLIONE SEMI-FREDDO

SERVES SIX

This comes from Osteria de' Poeti in Bologna. Though the recipe doesn't call for it, it's much easier to slice if you freeze it. My stepdaughter Olivia was so taken with it thats she's going to make it next time we have people round. I like cooking with her. She loves making desserts and wants to be a pastry cook. *Recipe photograph overleaf*

For the meringue
3 egg whites
170g caster sugar

For the zabaglione
5 egg yolks
75g caster sugar
100ml sweet Marsala
125ml double cream

To serve
400g fresh strawberries,
    hulled and sliced
1 tbsp aged balsamic vinegar
1 tbsp caster sugar

Heat the oven to 100°C/gas ¼. Line a baking sheet of at least 24cm x 33cm with baking parchment.

Make the meringue: whisk the egg whites until you have soft peaks, then add half the sugar and continue to whisk. Add the rest of the sugar and whisk to fairly stiff peaks. Spread into a thin layer of about 24cm by 33cm on the lined baking sheet. Bake for 2 hours.

Make the zabaglione by whisking the egg yolks and sugar in a large, heatproof bowl (the mixture expands) until fairly thick and pale, then set over a pan of simmering water and continue to whisk for about 5 minutes until really thick. Start adding the Marsala a little at a time, whisking well between additions. You want the mixture to be as thick as possible. When all the Marsala has been incorporated, take off the heat and set aside. Lightly whip the cream to the same consistency as the zabaglione, then fold the two together.

Line a 25cm x 12cm loaf tin with 2 sheets of clingfilm placed at right angles to each other and with the excess overhanging the sides. Cut the meringue into 3 equal rectangles of about 24cm x 11cm and place one in the bottom of the tin. Then spoon in half of the zabaglione, top with another layer of meringue and the rest of the zabaglione, and finally top with the third piece of meringue. Fold the clingfilm over the top and wrap the whole thing in a final sheet. Freeze for at least 5 hours, preferably overnight.

About 15 minutes before serving, combine the strawberries, balsamic vinegar and sugar in a bowl and toss briefly. Set aside to marinate.

To serve, remove the semi-freddo from the freezer, turn out of the loaf tin on to a plate and unpeel the clingfilm. Cut into slices using a serrated knife and serve at once with the marinated strawberries.

SMASHED LIQUORICE MERINGUES
WITH BERRIES & CHOCOLATE CREAM

=== SERVES SIX TO EIGHT ===

This is a very Icelandic combination; they love liquorice and chocolate. If you love liquorice, go for 2½ teaspoons of the liquorice powder. If you are unsure, go for a more conservative entry-level single teaspoon.

4 egg whites
Pinch salt
200g caster sugar
1–2½ tsp liquorice powder
   (see introduction)
½ tsp black food colouring
   (optional)
500ml double cream
225g chocolate
   (70 per cent cocoa solids),
   200g chopped,
   25g for shavings
150g fresh raspberries
100g fresh redcurrants

Heat the oven to 100°C/gas ¼. Line a baking sheet with baking parchment.

Place the egg whites and salt in a large metal bowl and, using an electric whisk, begin whisking on medium speed. When you reach soft floppy peak stage, add a third of the sugar and the liquorice powder. Keep whisking, and when incorporated add another third, then the final third, and bring together to a fairly stiff glossy mixture. If using food colouring, stir through to give a marble effect.

Dollop the mixture into piles on the lined baking sheet. Bake for about 1½ to 2 hours or until dry and crisp. Remove and cool. Store in an airtight tin if not using immediately.

Make a ganache. Scald 200ml of the double cream in a pan (bring just to the boil then take immediately off the heat) and pour it over the chopped chocolate in a bowl. Stir until the cream has melted. Allow to cool to room temperature; do not refrigerate.

When you are ready to serve, use a balloon whisk or electric beater to incorporate the remaining cream into the ganache. It tends to stiffen when left to stand, so make last minute for a light mousse-like texture.

To serve, dollop the chocolate cream along the centre of a large oval platter. Break up the meringues and scatter them over the top, along with the raspberries and redcurrants. Finish with chocolate shavings.

SUNDAY LUNCH

NAVARIN OF LAMB WITH FLAGEOLET BEANS 248

CHICKEN WITH STUFFING & GARLIC GRAVY FROM LA TUPINA 249

SALT PORK BELLY WITH SPLIT PEA PURÉE & SAUERKRAUT 252

TOPSIDE OF BEEF WITH HORSERADISH, APPLE SAUCE & ROSTI POTATOES 254

SPICED EINTOPF VENISON CASSEROLE WITH ROASTED PUMPKIN PURÉE 256

PORTUGUESE SEAFOOD RICE WITH PRAWNS, MUSSELS & CRAB 257

MUSSELS WITH BAYONNE HAM & SHALLOTS 260

DRESS THE BOARD SPATCHCOCKED CHICKEN 262

VEGETABLE STRUDEL 264

CALAMARI SOUVLAKI 265

When we started planning the TV programmes for *Long Weekends*, we thought about featuring Sunday lunch in one restaurant from each city in the series. It's a good time to get to know what the Bordelais, Viennese, Bolognese or Gaditanos of Cadiz are really like. There is something especially relaxing about a restaurant full of people on a Sunday. It's a time for families and, in the case of lunch in France, lots of dogs too. The image springs to mind of the Mussels with Bayonne Ham and Shallots on page 260, which I had on a sunny Sunday at a restaurant called Chez Hortense on Cap Ferret, about an hour from Bordeaux. It's a long, low, beach house fronted by grey-green sand-loving plants looking over the Arcachon basin towards the largest dune in Europe, the Dune du Pilat. It's very informal: a green and white-striped awning over the terrace and the same coloured wallpaper, scrubbed pine tables, and wood and rattan chairs. The scene that October Sunday was lots of animated families, lots of bottles of tannic and fresh Cru Bourgeois, crisp yellow *pommes frites* and steaming pots of *moules*. Nobody does Sunday lunch in a restaurant better than the French. The dishes I have brought back include things like a great roast chicken from La Tupina in Bordeaux with a stuffing of smoked bacon, garlic and chicken livers (page 249).

Turning to Berlin, I urge you to try the Salt Pork Belly with Split Pea Purée and Sauerkraut on page 252. It's my take on *Eisbein*, the famous boiled pork knuckle so loved by the Germans. It's crying out for a glass or two or red burgundy or, more correctly, *Spätburgunder*. Two or three Sundays ago I cooked the Portuguese Arroz de Marisco (page 257) for twelve people and it was very well received. I have written the recipe for four people because that's about as much as you can fit in a pan you might have at home, but I think it's worth getting hold of an extra-large frying pan, about 36cm across, for big occasions, or use a wider still but shallower paella pan. I also highly recommend the Viennese *Tafelspitz* (page 254), which is to the Austrians what roast beef and Yorkshire puddings are to us. In this case I think it would be a good idea to make it for four as a practice run, just to get the timings right before you up the numbers to eight or twelve. Turning now to an outdoor extravaganza for the summer, I recommend the Dress the Board Chicken on page 262. This would be the heart of an al fresco Sunday lunch. It's informal, there's no tricky last-minute procedure and all you need to accompany it are lots of lovely salads and bread.

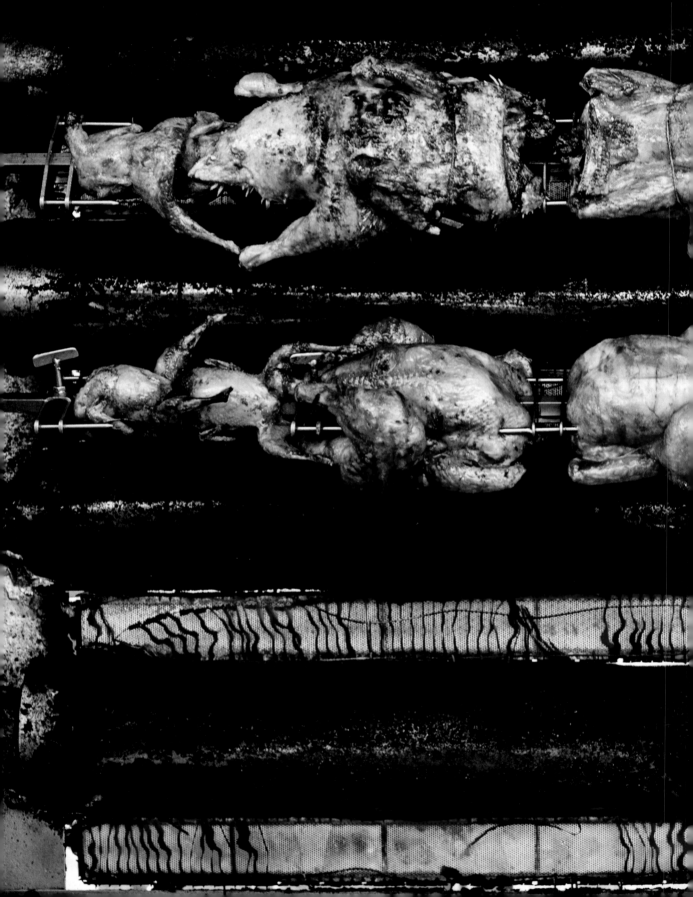

NAVARIN OF LAMB
WITH FLAGEOLET BEANS
SERVES FOUR TO SIX

I have to own up that for me Bordeaux was all about the wine. Second only to beef is a navarin of lamb with Bordeaux reds, particularly Graves. In my ideal weekend it is a dish for Saturday night, but since it is quite an easy dish the emphasis is on choosing the right wine to go with it. Here are a couple of suggestions given me by my son Charlie: St Nicolas-de-Bourgueil, 'Les Quarterons', Amirault, Loire, and Sarget de Gruaud Larose 2000. He's in the wine business and came filming with us in Graves, where we tasted about 256 wines, by the end of which I was complaining I couldn't taste a thing and that my mouth was like a prune. He claimed to be in full command of his taste buds – that's youth for you. You will need to soak dried flageolet beans in cold water the night before you start this recipe. If you forget, you can do a cheat's 'quick soak', whereby you bring the beans up to the boil for 10 minutes then leave them to soak for two hours in their cooking liquid, before draining and using in the recipe. Serve the navarin with fine green beans or buttered spinach.

225g dried flageolet beans, soaked overnight, or 400g tin flageolet beans
1kg trimmed spring lamb shoulder, cut in 3–4cm cubes
2 tbsp sunflower oil
50g butter
2 onions, sliced
4 cloves garlic, finely chopped or grated
3 carrots, cut into thick slices
1 tbsp tomato paste
2 tbsp plain flour
600ml *brown Chicken stock* (page 307)
Sprigs thyme
1 sprig rosemary
1½ tsp fine salt
6 turns black peppermill
12 small new potatoes, scrubbed, boiled for 5 minutes and drained
Small handful flat-leaf parsley, leaves chopped, to serve

Drain the soaked flageolet beans (if using) and place in a pan, cover with fresh water and bring to the boil, boil for 10 minutes, turn down to a simmer and cook for a further 30 minutes. Drain and set aside.

Heat a large flameproof casserole over high heat. Brown the lamb cubes all over in batches using a little of the butter and oil each time. Deglaze the pan with water between batches if required and reserve the deglazing liquid to add to the pot later. When all the lamb is browned, set aside.

Reduce the heat to medium, add the last of the butter and oil to the same pan and fry the onions until soft and golden, about 5 to 10 minutes, then add the garlic and carrots along with the tomato paste and flour and fry for another minute. Return the browned lamb together with the chicken stock, any deglazing juices, the flageolet beans (if using tinned flageolet beans add them a later on with the new potatoes) and the thyme, rosemary, salt and pepper. Bring to the boil, then turn down to a simmer and cook gently with a lid on for 1¼ hours. Add the new potatoes and cook for a further 10 to 15 minutes or until the meat, flageolet beans and potatoes are tender.

Remove the thyme and rosemary sprigs and check the seasoning. Scatter over the chopped parsley and serve.

CHICKEN WITH STUFFING & GARLIC GRAVY FROM LA TUPINA

≡ SERVES SIX ≡

Going to Bordeaux for my long weekend I had to revisit La Tupina. I've eaten there quite a few times over the years, and each new visit is always as good as the first: the côte de boeuf grilled on the open fire, the duck-fat chips, the chunky pâté known as *gratton*, and the miraculous wine list with so many good and inexpensive Bordeaux wines. It's all simple cooking and, for me, the sort of French food I will always love. I had a hankering for roast chicken this time. The stuffing, cooked separately, is especially satisfying.

Recipe photograph overleaf

1 x 2kg chicken
1 lemon, halved
1 tbsp olive oil
Salt and freshly ground
    black pepper
1 bulb garlic, separated
    into cloves
6 slices white bread
50g butter, softened
50ml white wine or water
Duck-fat chips (page 307),
    to serve

For the stuffing
10g butter
1 medium onion, chopped
10g garlic, chopped
350g minced pork
150g smoked bacon lardons
100g chicken livers
Sprig thyme, leaves picked
Handful flat-leaf parsley,
    roughly chopped
1 tsp fine salt
10 turns black peppermill

Heat the oven to 200°C/gas 6.

Rub the outside of the chicken with lemon, drizzle with the olive oil and season with salt and pepper. Bash the cloves of garlic to split (but not remove) their skins and put in the centre of a roasting tin. Place the chicken on top of the garlic. Roast the chicken for about 1½ hours or until a temperature probe indicates 75°C when inserted into the thickest part of the thigh, and the juices run clear.

Make the stuffing while the chicken is cooking. Melt the butter in a pan over medium heat, add the onion and garlic and sweat for about 5 to 10 minutes until softened. Set aside to cool a little. Put all the stuffing ingredients, including the onion and garlic, in a food processor and combine well. Roll the mixture into a long sausage about 7cm in diameter. Roll up in baking parchment and set aside in the fridge until ready to cook.

About 20 minutes before the chicken is ready, place the stuffing sausage, still wrapped in parchment, in the oven. Cook for about 35 minutes until the internal temperature reaches 75°C.

Meanwhile, when the chicken is cooked, remove to a carving plate/board and leave to rest, covered in tin foil, while you make the croutons and gravy. Use a pastry cutter to cut discs from the bread slices. Spread generously right to the edges with 30g of the butter. Fry gently in a frying pan or arrange on a tray in the oven and cook until crisp and golden brown.

Remove the garlic from the roasting tin and slip the skins off the cloves. Mash and set aside. Deglaze the pan with a little water or white wine on the hob and stir in the mashed garlic. Whisk in the remaining 20g butter and season with salt and pepper to taste. Carve the chicken and serve with a crouton alongside, topped with a slice of the stuffing and the garlic gravy.

SALT PORK BELLY *WITH* SPLIT PEA PURÉE & SAUERKRAUT

SERVES THREE TO FOUR

Much as I enjoyed ploughing through a boiled or roasted pig's knuckle in Germany, I think it's just a bit too local to reproduce outside the country. Really it's the combination of salt pork, sauerkraut and split peas that is so wonderful, so I've simply come up with gently simmering an unsmoked bacon joint with cloves, brown sugar, peppercorns and bay leaves. The quick-cook sauerkraut here is a short-cut to the real thing but, if you have time, a recipe for true fermented sauerkraut appears on page 309. If you can get some German mustard to serve alongside, so much the better.

600g unsmoked streaky
   bacon, in one piece,
   rind removed
1 onion, peeled and left whole
10 cloves
150ml cider
75g dark brown sugar
½ tsp chilli flakes
6 bay leaves, fresh if possible
1 tsp black peppercorns

For the quick-cook sauerkraut
1 tbsp olive oil
1 small onion, thinly sliced
1 medium white cabbage
   (about 750g), finely
   shredded
200ml cider vinegar
125ml cider
100ml water
1 tbsp fine salt
1 tsp caraway seeds

For the split pea purée
100ml rapeseed oil
1 onion, roughly chopped
2 cloves garlic, chopped
500g yellow split peas, rinsed
1.2 litres water
Juice 1 lemon
Salt and freshly ground
   black pepper

For the sauerkraut, heat the oil in a pan over medium-high heat and cook the onion, stirring, until it softens and turns translucent, 5 to 10 minutes. Add the cabbage, cider vinegar, cider, water, salt and caraway seeds and bring to the boil. Reduce the heat, cover and simmer for 45 minutes, until the cabbage is tender. Keep an eye on it. If it looks as if it is drying out, add a little water. Cool, then store in a sterilized glass Kilner jar. It will keep in the fridge for up to 2 weeks.

For the split pea purée, heat 2 to 3 tablespoons of the rapeseed oil in a large pan over medium heat, add the onion and garlic and sweat until soft and translucent, 5 to 10 minutes. Add the split peas and water, bring up to the boil and skim off any white scum that appears on the surface, then turn the heat down and simmer gently with a lid on the pan for 45 to 60 minutes, until thick and mushy. Add the remaining rapeseed oil and the lemon juice. Purée either in a food processor or using a stick blender. Season with salt and pepper. Set aside. If it thickens on standing, reheat with a little water.

Place the piece of bacon in a pan and cover with cold water. Stud the onion with the cloves and add to the pan with the cider, sugar, chilli flakes, bay leaves and peppercorns. Cover the pot and bring the water to the boil. Skim off any scum, reduce the heat and simmer for 45 to 60 minutes, until the meat is tender. Lift out of the cooking liquor with a slotted spoon and slice into about 6 to 8 long rashers. Serve with the split pea purée and sauerkraut.

TOPSIDE OF BEEF WITH HORSERADISH, APPLE SAUCE & RÖSTI POTATOES

SERVES EIGHT

My recipe for *Tafelspitz* comes from Plachutta, world-famous restaurant in the centre of Vienna. If you love your beef, this dish is a must. The name refers to the cut of meat known here as rump cap. I use very similar topside. I have adapted the dish to make it easy to serve at home. You need a large oven-to-table casserole. Put in the slices of beef, the vegetables, roasted marrowbone and cooking liquor, and serve everything else separately. It's a good idea to make the accompaniments during the two and a half hours' cooking time.

1 onion, halved through the root
2–3 litres water
1 tsp salt
2kg topside of beef
10 black peppercorns
800g mixed peeled root vegetables: carrots, swede, celeriac, cut into 4cm chunks
1 small leek, chopped into 4cm chunks
Chives, to finish

For the marrowbone
8 x 2cm-thick slices sawn marrowbone

For the rösti
800g waxy potatoes, such as Kipfler, boiled in their skins then grated
60g *Clarified butter* (page 309)

For the green vegetables
150–180ml water
250g frozen peas
Romaine lettuce, shredded
100g spinach
1 heaped tsp *Beurre manié* (page 309)
Salt and freshly ground black pepper

For the apple horseradish
2 Bramley apples, peeled, cored and chopped
4 tbsp creamed horseradish

To finish
4 slices rye bread, cut in half

Brown the onion well on the cut surface in a dry frying pan over medium heat. Set aside.

Bring the water to the boil with the salt in a large oven-to-table casserole pot over medium-high heat. Add the meat and bring back to the boil, then immediately turn down to a simmer. Skim off any scum that rises to the surface. Add the peppercorns and simmer gently for 2 hours. Add the root vegetables and leek and the browned onions and cook for a further 30 minutes.

Meanwhile, make the accompaniments. Heat the oven to 200°C/gas 6 and roast the marrowbone for 10–15 minutes.

For the rösti, melt the butter in large frying pan over medium heat and fry the grated potatoes until golden, about 7 to 10 minutes, then turn over and repeat on the other side.

For the green vegetables, bring the water to the boil, reduce the heat to medium and cook the peas for 5 minutes. Add the romaine lettuce and spinach and wilt for 2 to 3 minutes. Add the beurre manié, stir for 2 minutes then season with salt and pepper to taste.

Cook the Bramley apples in a splash of water for 10 minutes until pulpy and broken down. Stir into the horseradish.

To finish the main dish, lift the meat out of the liquid on to a cutting board. Cut into 1cm-thick slices and trim off any excess fat. Lift out the vegetables with a slotted spoon. Strain the liquid – this is to clear the stock – and return to the pan. Return the sliced meat and vegetables and add the marrowbone. Check the seasoning and reheat. Scatter with chives before serving. Bring to the table with all the accompaniments.

SPICED EINTOPF VENISON CASSEROLE WITH ROASTED PUMPKIN PURÉE

=== SERVES FOUR TO FIVE ===

'Eintopf' means cooked in one pot and, in this case, I suggest using a pleasant oven-to-table casserole. It is a particular type of German dish, which traditionally housewives used to prepare when they didn't have much time for cooking. This recipe came from one of our research trips to Berlin. It's the sort of thing any good chef would knock up without too much thought. What I especially liked about it was the Christmassy spice mix of cinnamon, nutmeg, juniper berries and cloves.

1 large onion, chopped
1 clove garlic, chopped
2 carrots, cut into rounds
2 sticks celery, finely sliced
2 tbsp olive oil
1 tbsp butter
1kg boned leg or shoulder
    of venison, cut into
    large chunks
Salt and freshly ground
    black pepper
3 tbsp plain flour
2 tbsp redcurrant
    or quince jelly
300ml red wine
500ml *Beef stock* (page 307)
100g cooked chestnuts
    (vacuum packed), halved
5 whole cloves
Large pinch freshly
    grated nutmeg
3 juniper berries,
    lightly crushed
6cm cinnamon stick
1 bay leaf

For the pumpkin purée
1kg pumpkin
2 tbsp olive oil
1 tsp salt
Freshly ground black pepper
25g butter

For the pumpkin purée, heat the oven to 180°C/gas 4. Cut the pumpkin in half and scrape out the seeds and stringy flesh. Place the pumpkin in a baking tray, drizzle with olive oil and season with the salt and pepper. Bake for 30 to 40 minutes until the flesh is tender. When cool enough to handle, scoop out the tender flesh and purée in a food processor or with a stick blender. Taste and adjust the seasoning and stir in the butter. Set aside.

Reduce the oven temperature to 150°C/gas 2.

In a heavy-based casserole over medium heat, fry the onion, garlic, carrot and celery in a little of the oil and butter until softened and golden, about 4 to 5 minutes. Remove with a slotted spoon and set aside.

Season the venison cubes with salt and pepper and toss in the flour. Add a little more oil and butter to the pan and fry the venison in batches, over high heat, until well browned. Set the meat aside.

Deglaze the pan with a little water, then taste the liquid. If burnt, discard; if good, keep. Add the redcurrant jelly and wine to the pan and bring to the boil. Pour in the beef stock, then return the meat and vegetables along with the chestnuts, cloves, nutmeg, juniper berries and cinnamon. Taste and season with salt and pepper and bring to the boil. Cover with a lid or tightly fitting foil and transfer to the oven for about 1½ hours or until tender.

Before serving, reheat the pumpkin/squash purée in a pan. Take the venison from the oven and check the seasoning; discard the cinnamon, cloves and bay leaves. Serve on top of the pumpkin purée.

PORTUGUESE SEAFOOD RICE
WITH PRAWNS, MUSSELS & CRAB

=== SERVES FOUR ===

I first tried this in Lisbon and concluded it was sort of a fish stew meets paella, and one which benefits from having a foot in both camps. On the fish-stew side, it is a lot moister than a paella, and on the paella-side it uses Arborio rice, which swells up, absorbing lots of delicious stock. Having suffered from too many dry and intense seafood paellas, I find *arroz de marisco* a refreshing change, particularly if you make it with a mixture of white and brown crab meat. It's as common in Portugal as risotto in Italy or paella in Spain, but while those dishes have strict rules attached to their making, *arroz* is very easy.

Recipe photograph overleaf

4 tbsp olive oil
1 large onion, chopped
2 cloves garlic,
   finely chopped
1 tsp sweet paprika
175ml dry white wine
2 large ripe tomatoes,
   deseeded and chopped
1 tbsp tomato paste
325g Arborio (risotto) rice
1.1–1.3 litres *Chicken* or
   Fish stock (page 307)
300g raw mussels, in
   the shell, scrubbed
275g raw king prawns,
   shells on
300g cooked crab meat,
   50/50 white and brown
1 tsp salt
8 turns black peppermill
Large pinch chilli flakes
Handful coriander,
   roughly chopped

To serve
1 lemon, cut into wedges
Crusty bread

Warm the olive oil in a large pan over medium heat. Sweat the onions and garlic until soft, about 5 minutes, then add the paprika and fry for 1 minute. Add the wine, tomatoes and tomato paste and simmer for about 5 minutes to reduce the liquid by half.

Stir in the rice and stock, cover the pan and simmer gently for about 12 minutes. Stir in the mussels and cook for a further 5 minutes, then add the prawns and cook until they have changed colour and the mussels have opened. Stir in the cooked crab meat. If the *arroz* looks too thick, loosen with a little more stock or water. It should be runny and not hold its shape. Season with salt, pepper, chilli flakes and coriander. Serve immediately with lemon wedges and crusty bread.

MUSSELS WITH BAYONNE HAM & SHALLOTS

SERVES THREE TO FOUR AS A STARTER

This recipe comes from a restaurant in Cap Ferrat called Chez Hortense, which is one of those destination restaurants where everyone seems to go for the same dish, with the essential accompaniment of a massive pile of pommes frites. I remember being filmed there remarking how well the quite humble Cru Bourgeois Bordeaux goes with it, partly because of the presence of salty cured ham. It is also a perfect opportunity to *faire chabrot*: to pour a little red wine into your dish after you have finished your mussels, stir it into the buttery, hammy juices, then tip the dish to your mouth and swallow. This dish is very quick to prepare and cook.

1.5kg raw mussels, scrubbed
2 tbsp dry white wine
50g butter
1 shallot, finely chopped
75g Bayonne or prosciutto
    ham, finely chopped
1 clove garlic, grated
    or finely chopped
Handful mixed flat-leaf
    parsley, tarragon, chervil
    and chives, chopped
Freshly ground black pepper
Crusty bread, to serve

Put the mussels in a large pan, add the white wine, cover and steam over high heat for about 3 to 4 minutes until opened, shaking the pan from time to time. Remove from the heat and strain into a colander set over a large bowl. Reserve the cooking liquor and keep the mussels warm.

In the pan, melt the butter and gently cook the shallots, ham and garlic for 4 to 5 minutes, until softened but not browned. Add the mussel cooking liquor, bring to the boil and reduce by half. Add the mussels and the herbs and mix well. Season with black pepper. Serve in warmed bowls with crusty bread.

DRESS *THE* BOARD SPATCHCOCKED CHICKEN

═ SERVES FOUR TO EIGHT ═

I got the idea for this recipe by watching a YouTube clip by Jamie Oliver, where he grilled a sirloin steak and let it rest on some herbs on a chopping board, allowing the juices from the steak to make a rudimentary sauce. It's the sort of impromptu cooking I love. I have taken the idea and used a Sicilian-inspired dressing of lemons, garlic, chilli, raisins, pine nuts, capers and oregano. I have tried this out a few times with friends at barbecues, and to keep things easy and controllable I roast the flattened chickens indoors first, then give them a charcoal flavour on the barbecue afterwards.

1 x 1.8–2kg chicken
2 cloves garlic, grated
  or finely chopped
2 tbsp olive oil
Zest and juice ½ lemon
Small handful flat-leaf
  parsley, chopped
½ tsp chilli flakes
1 tomato, finely chopped
10 pitted green olives,
  chopped
2 tsp pine nuts, toasted
2 tsp raisins
1 tbsp chopped capers
½ tsp dried oregano
½ tsp salt
12 turns black peppermill

Heat the oven to 200°C/gas 6.

Spatchcock the chicken by placing it on a board breast-side down, then, using poultry shears or good heavy scissors, cut down either side of the backbone, remove it and discard. Turn the board over and press down to flatten the chicken.

Place the chicken in a tin and roast for about 40 to 50 minutes, until the internal temperature is 70°C and the juices run clear. If you like, transfer to a barbecue for a few minutes to flavour and colour the meat.

Combine all the other ingredients in a bowl. When the chicken is cooked, remove from the roasting tin, pour off any excess fat and add the contents of the bowl. Put the chicken back in the tin on top, skin-side up, cover with foil and leave to rest for 5 to 10 minutes.

Transfer the chicken to a carving board or slice and serve on individual plates, spooning over the contents of the roasting tin.

GEMÜSESTRUDEL
VEGETABLE STRUDEL
SERVES FOUR TO SIX

Quite often really good dishes come my way when I am not looking for them. We were in Café Sperl filming a piece about what a convivial place a Viennese café is, where you can sit and read a newspaper all morning with a coffee and nobody will disturb you. After I'd done my piece to camera, most of the film crew ordered beef and gravy. In view of the enormous number of dishes I have to try, I had a simple chicken noodle soup. As is often the case with me, I looked at the nice beef with envy, but particularly interesting was the side dish of green vegetables in crisp strudel pastry. Eventually I asked Martin, the second cameraman, if he'd mind if I had a tiny piece of his. He agreed, and I am afraid I ate half of it, it was so good. You might consider serving this with roast beef and Yorkshire puddings on a Sunday.

100g butter
1 onion, chopped
2 carrots, finely chopped
250g spinach
1 small head of broccoli,
    broken into florets
½ tsp salt
12 turns black peppermill
5 large sheets filo pastry

In a large frying pan over medium heat, melt 30g of the butter and sweat the onion until soft, about 5 to 10 minutes. Add the carrots and fry for about 5 minutes until softened a little. Add the spinach and cook for 2 minutes until wilted. In a separate pan steam the broccoli for 3 minutes until just tender. Combine all the vegetables in a bowl, season with the salt and pepper and allow to cool.

Heat the oven to 190°C/Gas 5. Melt the remaining butter (70g).

On a clean, dry tea towel, layer the sheets of filo, one on top of the other, brushing each layer with melted butter. Arrange the vegetable filling along the length of the centre, leaving 5cm clear at the ends. Pull over the filo from the sides to cover the filling, then brush with butter to seal. Tuck the ends in, and carefully roll on to a baking sheet, seam-side down. Brush liberally with the remaining melted butter and bake for 20 to 25 minutes until crisp and golden.

CALAMARI SOUVLAKI

This recipe comes from a great seafood restaurant, Tsirikos Taverna at Nea Potidea on the Kassandra peninsula, just east of Thessaloniki. It is at a small marina and serves mostly boat owners and locals, in other words it is not particularly touristy. Every morning the owner and chef, Mikhalis, can be seen walking over to the boats to choose his fish for the day. The boats won't sell their catch until he has chosen. What I like about this dish, besides its simplicity, is the smell of squid and tomatoes on a barbecue, which even in a back garden in damp England smells of holidays.

Recipe photograph overleaf

600g squid, cleaned
  bodies and tentacles
½ tsp salt
Small handful fresh dill,
  roughly chopped
1 large or 2 small red peppers,
  seeded and cut into squares
3 large tomatoes, cut into
  chunks
2 tbsp olive oil
1½ tsp dried oregano
1 tbsp chopped flat-leaf
  parsley
Large pinch chilli flakes
Salt and freshly ground
  black pepper
1 lemon, cut into wedges,
  to serve

Cut the squid bodies into pieces about 3cm long. Put the body and tentacles in a bowl and sprinkle with the salt and chopped dill.

Thread the squid, including the tentacles, on to 8 metal or pre-soaked wooden skewers, alternating with the pepper and tomato. Brush with olive oil. Grill for 4 or 5 minutes on each side on a barbecue or under a hot grill.

Once cooked and charred at the edges, sprinkle with oregano, parsley, chilli flakes and salt and pepper, and serve with lemon wedges.

SUNDAY
NIGHT

'Strange how the night moves with autumn closing in'
BOB SEGER

Do you suffer from Sunday night blues, especially at the start of a new school year in September? Summer with the kids has been fabulous but you have to buy school uniforms, your tan is fading, one child is going to a new school, and there's that chill in the air with autumn closing in. That's the way I often feel on Sunday nights. When I used to cook for my sister and friends for a weekend at Trevose in the 1970s they'd either just left on Sunday afternoon or were going in the morning and I always felt melancholic. One way round it was to cook something simple and comforting, throwing myself into the task to alleviate the blues. I'd put some nice music on, have one last glass of wine and I'd be all right again. In a world where you can spend an awful lot of money having pins stuck into you or talking to a therapist about how wretched you feel, it seems to me that creating something personal to you by cooking is a very good way of cheering yourself up.

I think my father, who was something of a depressive, realized that. In my memoir *Under a Mackerel Sky* I wrote about the tomato and onion soup he used to make on a Sunday night with a stock made from the Sunday roast chicken, still a calm memory for me. The Caldo Verde, Portuguese kale soup, on page 277 is in the same vein. I first tasted it in a fado bar in Lisbon, enjoying spoonfuls of its comfort while listening to a full-bosomed girl sing about the sadness of love. Sunday night, too, would be a good time to make Tortelloni with Ricotta, Butter and Sage (page 289). Making tortelloni requires a little skill, but not much. You can just sit at the kitchen table making them and listening to some music. They are stuffed with ricotta, nutmeg and lemon zest, boiled for about 3 minutes and tossed with melted butter, sage and Parmesan. I am not suggesting you make the Anelletti alla Palermitana (page 292) – baked pasta hoops with minced pork, beef aubergine, basil and tomato – on Sunday night. It's something you would have made earlier, but reheated and served with the warm salad from Bologna – Spinach and Parmesan with Pancetta Cooked in Balsamic Vinegar on page 284 – and a modest glass of, shall we say, Primitivo, and then the dark spirits hovering around you will disappear up the chimney or under the door.

SARMA
PICKLED CABBAGE LEAVES STUFFED *WITH* SMOKED HAM, PORK & CARAWAY SEEDS

=== SERVES THREE TO FOUR ===

Sarma probably originated in Turkey; there are versions all over Greece, Romania, Bulgaria, Serbia and Croatia. I have had it many times in Greece, but what makes this recipe so special is the fact that the cabbage leaves are pickled like sauerkraut. The owner and chef of Zur Herknerin, Stefanie Herkner, who made this for me, explained that it was also a traditional Viennese recipe, and her version was always cooked by her grandmother and mother. I don't know if it was because this was an intrinsically good recipe or more that Stefanie was such a lovely person, but it was one of my favourites of all my long weekends.

6 large or 8 medium *Pickled cabbage leaves* (page 309), plus scraps

For the filling
30g lard
1 onion, chopped
1 large carrot, finely grated
500g minced pork
60g speck, finely chopped
1 tsp sweet paprika
½ tsp salt
10 turns black peppermill
75g long-grain rice
150ml water
1 egg, beaten

For cooking
3 cloves garlic, chopped
½ tsp black peppercorns
4 bay leaves
½ tsp sweet paprika
750ml–1 litre water

To serve
16–20 new potatoes, skin on
20g butter
½ tsp caraway seeds
Salt and freshly ground black pepper
Small handful flat-leaf parsley, chopped
100ml sour cream

Heat the lard in a frying pan over medium heat, add the onion and carrot and sweat them for 7 to 10 minutes. Add the minced pork and speck, season with the paprika, salt and pepper and cook for 20 minutes until browned.

Stir in the rice and water, then cover and cook for 8 to 10 minutes to part-cook the rice. Allow to cool and mix in the beaten egg. Spoon the filling into the middle of each leaf, fold in the sides and roll up.

Put half the scraps of pickled cabbage over the base of a large shallow casserole or pan with a lid. Arrange the stuffed leaves on top, fold-side down. Add the garlic, peppercorns, bay leaves, paprika, the remaining scraps, and enough water to barely cover the leaves. Cover the pan and cook gently over low-medium heat for 30 to 40 minutes.

Boil the potatoes until tender, about 15 minutes, then drain and, when cool enough to handle, slip the skins off. Heat the butter in a pan over medium heat, add the caraway seeds and the potatoes and roll around until well coated and warmed through. Season with salt and pepper, then remove from the heat and sprinkle with chopped parsley.

Lift the rolls out with a slotted spoon and serve warm, topped with sour cream and with the potatoes on the side.

COTOLETTA ALLA BOLOGNESE
VEAL CUTLET BOLOGNESE STYLE
≡ SERVES FOUR ≡

This has a slightly 1970s feel to it. You might want a candle in a raffia-covered Chianti bottle on the table when you eat it.

4 x 150g slices veal rump
Salt and freshly ground
    black pepper
60g plain flour
2 eggs, beaten
120g dried white
    Breadcrumbs (page 309)
40g butter
6 tbsp olive oil
8 slices prosciutto
100g Parmesan cheese,
    shaved into slivers
100ml *Chicken stock*
    (page 307)
Sauté potatoes
    (page 308), to serve

Place the veal slices between sheets of clingfilm and beat, using a meat mallet or rolling pin, until about 3–5mm thick. Season the escalopes with salt and pepper. Set up 3 plates, 1 with flour, 1 with beaten egg and 1 with breadcrumbs. Coat each escalope on both sides first in flour, then egg, then breadcrumbs. Set aside.

Heat the butter and olive oil in a large frying pan, for which you have a lid or a baking sheet to cover, over a high heat until foaming. Fry the escalopes for 3 minutes on each side. If there is a lot of fat left in the pan, pour most of it away. Top each escalope in the pan with 2 slices of prosciutto and 25g of the cheese. Pour in the chicken stock and cover with a lid. Continue to cook for 3 to 5 minutes until the cheese has melted.

If the pan is not big enough to accommodate 4 escalopes, you can transfer the cooked escalopes and stock to an oven dish, cover with foil and cook at 180°C/gas 4 for 4 to 5 minutes or until the cheese has melted.

Serve immediately with sauté potatoes.

CALDO VERDE
GREEN KALE SOUP
WITH CHORIZO & POTATO
═ SERVES FOUR ═

Will our new-found love for chorizo ever fade, I wonder. In my memoir *Under a Mackerel Sky* I wrote about my friend at Oxford, Martin Leeburn, who appeared at our student house in the early 1970s with a couple of chorizo sausages; he'd been to Spain for a year as a language student. I never got over it. Portuguese *chouriço* is just as good, and it's the secret of *caldo verde*. It's the combination of smoky, *pimentão*-flavoured sausage and garlic, with good, potato-thickened stock and the brilliant green and slightly bitter kale that makes this peasant dish unforgettable. I have to own up to slightly jazzing the dish up with chilli flakes and extra chorizo. In Portugal they grow a specific type of kale for this soup, very much like our collard greens. It's also the grelos used in Galicia for a pork and greens stew called *cocido gallego*. The Portuguese slice the greens very thinly using a special slicer but I prefer thicker strips. *Recipe photograph overleaf*

1 onion, finely chopped
1 large clove garlic,
    finely chopped
1 x 225g chorizo or *chouriço*
    (sausage), cut into chunks
3 tbsp olive oil
400g potatoes, preferably
    floury, peeled and cut
    into 3cm chunks
1.75 litres water or
    Vegetable stock (page 307)
300g spring greens or kale,
    finely shredded
1 tsp salt
6 turns black peppermill
Large pinch chilli flakes

Fry the onion, garlic and chorizo or *chouriço* in the olive oil in a large pan over medium heat until the onions and garlic are soft and translucent, 5 to 8 minutes. Add the potatoes and the stock and let this boil until the potatoes are cooked, about 10 minutes.

Pulverize the potatoes in the broth with a potato masher. Add the kale, bring back to the boil and simmer for 4 to 5 minutes until the kale is cooked but still a vibrant green. Season with salt and pepper and serve in warmed bowls with chilli flakes sprinkled on top.

VEFA'S LAMB CASSEROLE
WITH AUBERGINE
=== SERVES SIX ===

When I was in Thessaloniki I drove an hour to Halkidiki beach to Vefa Alexiadou's house overlooking the bay. Her book *Vefa's Kitchen* is to Greece what Delia Smith's *Complete Cookery* is to us. Like Delia she had a highly successful career on TV. I asked her what the secret of her TV success was, to which she replied, 'People love me.' You gotta love the Greeks. She was very good news and cooked a rather more elaborate version of this dish for me, but admitted that at home this simpler one was what she went for.

2kg aubergines,
    sliced 5mm thick
2 red peppers,
    seeded and sliced
1½ tsp salt
250ml olive oil
1.5kg boneless shoulder
    of lamb, trimmed of fat
    and cut into 3cm pieces
1 large onion, finely chopped
4 cloves garlic, chopped
    or grated
2 x 400g tins chopped
    tomatoes
1 tbsp tomato paste
1 tsp sugar
1 large handful parsley,
    roughly chopped
500ml water, plus extra
    if needed
20 turns black peppermill

Sprinkle the aubergine and red pepper with a third of the salt and leave to drain in a colander for half an hour. Remove and dry in a tea towel.

Heat the olive oil in a casserole over medium heat, add the aubergine and pepper and cook, turning occasionally, until lightly browned, about 10 minutes. Remove with a slotted spoon and set aside.

Add the meat to the casserole and cook over medium heat, stirring frequently, until nicely coloured, about 8 minutes. Add the onion and garlic and cook for a further 4 minutes. Add the chopped tomatoes, tomato paste, sugar, parsley, water, the remaining salt and the pepper, cover and simmer for 1½ to 2 hours, until the meat is tender and the sauce is thick. Add extra water during this time if the stew becomes too dry.

Heat the oven to 200°C/gas 6.

Return the aubergines and red peppers to the pan, folding them through the stew a little. Transfer to the hot oven and bake for 20 minutes.

FARFALLE WITH PEAS & PANCETTA

SERVES FOUR TO SIX

This is a memory for me of a glorious lunch at the house of Rita Mattioli in Bologna. Rita teaches people to cook in her lovely top-floor apartment in a palazzo in the town centre. She actually made this with her homemade *garganelli*. This is a small roll of pasta marked with a grooved wooden spatula, the idea being that it holds sauce better. This pasta is difficult to get outside of Bologna so I make it with farfalle instead. It's dead simple: pancetta, peas and loads of Parmesan – lovely. *Recipe photograph overleaf*

For the pasta
300g 00 pasta flour,
　plus extra for dusting
½ tsp salt, plus extra
　for cooking
3 eggs, beaten

For the sauce
100g shallots, finely chopped
30g butter
200g pancetta, chopped
　into matchstick strips
500g frozen petits pois
1 bay leaf
Sprig thyme
400ml *Vegetable* or *Chicken*
　stock (page 307)
70g Parmesan cheese, freshly
　grated, plus extra to serve
10 turns black peppermill
Salt, to taste

Make the pasta by combining the flour, salt and eggs in a food processor to 'breadcrumb' stage, then tip out on to a lightly floured board and knead for 3 to 4 minutes until smooth and elastic. Form into a ball, wrap in clingfilm and allow to rest for at least 30 minutes before rolling.

Roll out the pasta and cut into strips 4cm wide, ideally using a wavy-edged pastry cutter. Then, using a knife, cut into at 5–6cm intervals into rectangles. Take the centre of each rectangle between your fingers and pleat and pinch to form a bow. Set aside to dry while you make the sauce.

Sweat the shallots in the butter over medium for about 4 to 5 minutes or until soft. Add the pancetta and cook for 3 to 4 minutes, then add the peas, bay leaf, thyme and stock, reduce the heat and simmer for 10 to 15 minutes.

Cook the farfalle in boiling salted water for 3 to 4 minutes until tender. Stir the grated Parmesan into the pea sauce. Taste and season with the pepper, and salt if required. Drain the pasta well and add to the sauce. Stir well to combine and serve immediately with more freshly grated Parmesan.

SPINACH & PARMESAN SALAD
WITH PANCETTA COOKED IN BALSAMIC VINEGAR

=== SERVES TWO ===

I had this spinach salad wilted with hot pancetta, balsamic and Parmesan as a side order in the Trattoria dal Biassanot. I thought it was very grown-up.

4 slices pancetta, chopped
1 tsp olive oil, for frying (optional)
3 tbsp balsamic vinegar
120g baby spinach, washed and spun
60g Parmesan cheese, shaved into slivers
2 tbsp olive oil, to serve

Fry the pancetta in a small frying pan over a medium-high heat until it starts to crisp, about 1 or 2 minutes. Use the teaspoon of olive oil if the pancetta is not fatty enough to fry on its own. Add the balsamic vinegar and reduce it until it just glazes the pancetta.

Pile the baby spinach on plates, add the pancetta, cover with slivers of Parmesan and drizzle with the 2 tablespoons of olive oil.

PASTA ALLA PESTO TRAPANESE
PASTA WITH AN ALMOND, BASIL & PECORINO PESTO

SERVES SIX

Although this dish originated in Trapani, it is found everywhere in Palermo. Trapanese pesto is usually made with almonds and tomatoes, not pine nuts. I have written this for spaghetti, linguine or bucatini but quite often in Sicily it's made with busiate, a long, corkscrew-shaped pasta, sadly near impossible to find in the UK. Vegetarian pasta dishes like this are so much a part of Sicilian cuisine.

75g whole almonds
Large handful torn basil (30g)
4 cloves garlic, chopped
300g cherry tomatoes, halved
50g pecorino cheese, grated, plus extra to serve
6 tbsp olive oil
8 turns black peppermill
½ tsp salt, plus extra for cooking
500g spaghetti, linguine or bucatini

Blanch the almonds in boiling water for a few minutes to loosen their skins, then pinch off the skins with your fingers when the nuts are cool enough to handle. Toast the skinned almonds in a dry frying pan over medium-high heat. Keep them moving to prevent burning; you are aiming for a light golden colour.

In a food processor, pulse the almonds until they resemble breadcrumbs. Put aside a few of the basil leaves for decoration, then add the rest of the basil and the garlic to the almonds, and pulse a couple of times to combine. Tip into a bowl.

Mix the tomatoes into the almond, basil and garlic mixture, and stir in the grated cheese and olive oil. Taste and season with pepper and salt.

Boil the pasta in plenty of salted water, drain when al dente (follow packet instructions), add the pesto and stir through. Garnish with basil and serve with plenty of additional pecorino.

VRUOCCULI AFFUCATI
SICILIAN 'DROWNED' CAULIFLOWER

Drowned this Sicilian cauliflower indeed is – in red wine. I thought of making this recipe for a photograph but the cauliflower doused in red wine looks a bit unappetizing. However, it is absolutely delicious, particularly because of the bold flavours of pecorino, anchovies and olives. It also has the advantage of being very easy to make.

60ml olive oil
20g tinned anchovies,
    drained and chopped
6 spring onions, finely sliced
600g Romanesco cauliflower,
    in small florets
75g pecorino cheese,
    cut into 4–5mm dice
16 pitted black olives, halved
¼ tsp salt
10 turns black peppermill
200ml red wine

In a good-sized saucepan for which you have a lid, put half the olive oil, a third of the anchovies, a third of the spring onions, a third of the cauliflower florets and a third of the pecorino dice.

Now add half the olives and another third of anchovies, spring onions, cauliflower and pecorino. Add another layer of the same, then press down to compress.

Sprinkle with the salt and pepper and pour over the remaining olive oil and the red wine. Put a lid on the pan, place over medium heat and bring up to a simmer. Reduce the heat and cook gently for 20 to 25 minutes until the cauliflower has taken on a pink hue and is tender.

TORTELLONI *WITH* RICOTTA, BUTTER & SAGE

This is a perfect Sunday evening dish. It is not nearly as fiddly as you might think, and there is something therapeutic about making it. Light, full of flavour and comforting.

For the pasta
200g 00 pasta flour,
    plus extra for dusting
½ tsp salt
2 eggs

For the filling
150g ricotta
50g Parmesan cheese, grated
Few rasps nutmeg
1 egg yolk
½ tsp salt
5 turns black peppermill
Zest ½ small lemon

To serve
50g butter
6 sage leaves, torn
75g Parmesan cheese, grated

Make the pasta by combining the flour, salt and eggs in a food processor to 'breadcrumb' stage, then tip out on to a lightly floured board and knead for 3 to 4 minutes until smooth and elastic. Form into a ball, wrap in clingfilm and allow to rest for at least 30 minutes before rolling.

Roll the pasta into sheets about 2mm thick. Cut into 5cm-wide strips, then cut across into squares.

Mix the filling ingredients together and spoon scant teaspoonfuls of the mixture into the centre of each pasta square. Fold the pasta corner to corner to make a triangle with the filling encased. Press to seal the edges, then wrap each triangle around your little finger and pinch the points together. Curl the uppermost point backwards to give the classic tortelloni shape.

Bring a large pan of salted water to the boil and boil the tortelloni for about 3 minutes, then drain. Melt the butter in a frying pan and add the sage leaves. Add the cooked tortelloni and toss to coat in the butter, then remove from the heat and add the grated Parmesan. Serve immediately.

ANELLETTI ALLA PALERMITANA
BAKED PASTA ⟍with⟍ A BEEF, PORK & TOMATO RAGÙ

=== SERVES SIX ===

To think I have been alive all these years and never come across *anelletti alla palermitana*. I suppose you could call it Sicily's answer to lasagne, but with its filling of pork and beef, red wine, fried aubergine, pecorino and the distinctive hoop-shaped pasta, it's also completely different. It comes in two versions in shops in Palermo: either a loose pasta with sauce or, as in this case, baked in a springform tin, which allows you to slice it and have it cold for a picnic. I actually prefer it baked like this and served straight from the oven. Even though it doesn't entirely hold its shape, it has a delicious and unusual density to it.

120ml olive oil
1 onion, finely chopped
1 clove garlic, finely chopped
2 carrots, finely chopped
1 stick celery, finely chopped
250g minced beef
150g minced pork
150ml red wine
Small handful fresh basil
450ml *Tomato sauce*
  (page 308)
2 tbsp tomato paste
1 tsp salt
8 turns black peppermill
350g anelletti (O-shaped
  pasta) or macaroni
Salt, for cooking
1 aubergine, cut into 1cm dice
20g butter, softened,
  for greasing
30g dried white *Breadcrumbs*
  (page 309)
50g pecorino cheese, grated

Heat 50ml of the olive oil in a saucepan over medium heat. Fry the onion, garlic, carrot and celery for 10 minutes. Add the beef and pork and brown for 5 to 10 minutes. Add the red wine, reduce by half, then add the basil and tomato sauce and paste. Simmer for 30 minutes until you have a rich ragù. Season with the salt and pepper.

Boil the anelletti until three-quarters cooked, about 8 minutes, in plenty of salted water with a dash of olive oil (10ml). It should still retain a bit of bite, as it will continue to cook in the oven. Drain well and mix with the ragù.

In a frying pan over medium-high heat, warm the remaining 70ml olive oil and fry the aubergine dice for about 3 to 5 minutes until golden. Drain on kitchen paper and stir into the pasta and ragu.

Heat the oven to 190°C/gas 5.

Butter a 23cm springform cake tin and sprinkle the base and sides with half the breadcrumbs and pecorino. Spoon in the pasta. Finish with the remaining breadcrumbs mixed with pecorino. Press down firmly with the back of a wooden spoon. Bake for about 25 to 30 minutes until the top has taken on a bit of colour and formed a crust. Serve warm with a side salad or, for a picnic, allow to cool in the tin and refrigerate. When cold, run a knife around the edge and remove the ring. Cut into wedges and serve with a salad.

GURNARD WITH LENTILS & PASSATELLI

Ristorante Ciacco was just across the road from my hotel in Bologna. That's Bologna for you: the centre is so compact that most of the restaurants are just around the corner. It's a bit like Venice in this respect, lots of very narrow streets that seem to be endless when in fact you are just walking around in circles feeling very medieval. This is a common Italian way with fish and pasta. The fillets are cut up into small pieces and fried in olive oil and garlic, then tossed with pasta. In this case the lentils give it an extra earthiness, and the passatelli, made with Parmesan and lots of eggs, enrich the dish.

2 tbsp olive oil,
  plus extra to serve
1 clove garlic, unpeeled
  and bashed
350g gurnard fillet,
  cut into 2cm pieces
Salt, to taste
5 turns black peppermill
100ml *Fish stock* (page 307)
Small bunch flat-leaf
  parsley, chopped

For the lentils
2 tbsp olive oil
1 clove garlic, chopped
½ banana shallot,
  finely chopped
½ small carrot,
  finely chopped
½ small stick celery,
  finely chopped
50g green continental
  or Puy lentils
½ tsp oregano or thyme
Salt and freshly ground
  black pepper

For the passatelli
200g dried white
  Breadcrumbs (page 309)
200g Parmesan
  cheese, grated
3 eggs, beaten
6–8 rasps freshly
  grated nutmeg
Zest 1 lemon

First prepare the lentils. In a pan over medium heat, warm the olive oil and add the garlic, shallot, carrot and celery and cook until softened, 5 to 10 minutes. Rinse the lentils in cold water, drain and add to the pan with enough water to cover – about 300–350ml – and the oregano or thyme. Season with salt and pepper. Simmer for about 20 to 25 minutes until tender but not mushy. Set aside.

In a food processor, mix all the passatelli ingredients into a ball of dough, wrap in cling film and rest for 20 minutes.

Put a large pan of salted water on to boil.

Heat the olive oil in a frying pan over medium heat. Add the garlic clove and allow to infuse the oil for about 30 seconds, then remove from the pan. Add the chunks of gurnard and fry for 2 minutes. Season with salt and pepper. Add 4 to 5 tablespoons of the lentils (keep any remaining in the fridge to add to a salad) and the fish stock and cook down for 1 to 2 minutes, while you finish the passatelli

Pass the passatelli dough through a ricer into the boiling water. When the noodles rise to the surface they are cooked; this takes about a minute. Drain and add to the pan with the parsley and a drizzle of olive oil. Toss gently to mix, taking care not to break up the fish or the passatelli, and serve at once.

WARM POTATO SALAD WITH TUNA

I ate this at a tapas bar called Barbiana in Sanlúcar de Barrameda, made with the thickest, bitterest, green olive oil and the nuttiest sherry vinegar, and sweet warm new potatoes, soft sliced onions, parsley and a topping of locally tinned melva tuna – it's this kind of dish, so simple and so dependent on the quality of every ingredient, that makes the cooking of this glorious part of Andalusia so special.

500g new potatoes
½ small onion, very
   finely chopped
1 tbsp flat-leaf parsley,
   roughly chopped
3 tbsp olive oil
1½ tbsp sherry vinegar
¼ tsp sea salt
200g tinned tuna steak
   in olive oil

Cook the potatoes in their skins until tender, about 30 minutes. Drain and, when cool enough to handle, peel them and cut them roughly in half. Place in a bowl and add the onion and parsley. Dress with 2 tablespoons of the olive oil and all the vinegar.

Arrange the dressed potatoes on a plate or shallow bowl and drizzle over the remaining olive oil. Sprinkle with the sea salt. Add large pieces of tuna and serve immediately.

VIENNESE HERRING SALAD

≡ SERVES FOUR ≡

Martina Hohenlohe is the editor-in-chief for Gault et Millau in Austria. I met her at the Hotel Imperial in Vienna, where she had fixed up an opportunity for me to watch the definitive Wiener Schnitzel being made (page 198). During my conversation she gave me her book *Viennese Cuisine*, and I noticed this recipe for herring salad. Of course, cured herrings are available all over Europe, even in the most landlocked countries, such as Austria. I particularly liked the fact that the salad comes with potato and apple, cannellini beans and hard-boiled egg. It is a lovely dish. I am proud to say that Martina and her husband will be coming to Padstow and dining at our restaurant.

500g new potatoes, skin on
200g marinated
    herring, drained
80g tinned cannellini
    beans, drained
1 tbsp capers
2 apples, Granny Smith
    or Cox's Orange, peeled,
    cored and sliced
1 onion, finely chopped
80g pickled gherkins, sliced
150ml sour cream
2 tbsp *Mustard mayonnaise*
    (page 308)
2 tsp cider vinegar
1 tsp horseradish cream or
    freshly grated horseradish
1 anchovy fillet, crushed
    to a paste
1 tsp Dijon mustard
½ tsp salt
4 turns black peppermill

To serve
1 egg, hard-boiled and sliced
Few sprigs fresh dill,
    roughly chopped

Cook the potatoes in their skins until tender, about 10 to 15 minutes. When cool enough to handle, slip off the skins and dice the flesh. Chop the herrings into similar-sized pieces. In a large bowl, combine the herring, potatoes, cannellini beans, capers, apple, onion and gherkins.

Make the mayonnaise in a bowl by mixing the egg yolk with mustard, lemon juice and salt, then gradually add the vegetable oil, stirring continuously, until all the oil in incorporated.

In a bowl, mix the sour cream, vinegar, horseradish, anchovy, mustard, salt and pepper. Add 2 tablespoons of the mayonnaise. Use to dress the herring mixture. Leave for 30 minutes before serving, decorated with the slices of hard-boiled egg and the chopped dill.

TRAVEL INFORMATION

BORDEAUX

EATING OUT: La Tupina for Côte de Boeuf (page 184), roast chicken (page 249) and *gratton* with radishes; **Le Petit Commerce**, a good fish restaurant right in the centre, for fillet of *maigre* (corvina); **Chez Hortense**, at Cap Ferrat, for Mussels with Bayonne Ham (page 260); the **Grand Hotel** for really posh Sole à la Meunière (page 194) and a good place to stay. For a nice village bistro and all the smartest chateaux nearby, try the **Bistrot 'Chez Mémé'** at Saint-Julienne-Beychevelle. There is a very good fish restaurant at Arcachon, **Chez Pierre**, and the cutting-edge **Garopapilles** in Bordeaux. A great place for breakfast is **La Tupina** café, right on the Garonne. Try to get out to Saint-Émilion for Sunday lunch; it's really pretty. I like the **Logis de la Cadène** – try to book a table on the terrace if it's warm.

SHOPPING: A visit to the central market, the **Marché des Capuchins**, is a must. A wonderful cheese shop is **Jean d'Alos**, where the underground cellars have been used for ageing cheese for thirty-four years. There's an incredible wine shop next to the Grand Hotel, **L'Intendent**. For the best vintage, stick to the 'rule of five': every fifth year from 1985 ending in a '5' or '0' is a great one. My friends' Gavin and Angela Quinney's good, every-day Bordeaux is available from **Château Bauduc**.

WHERE TO STAY: If you fancy pampering, you'll enjoy **Les Sources de Caudalie** at Château Smith Haut Lafitte. For a slightly wacky luxury hotel, with a Harley-Davidson in the bedroom, try **Le Saint-James**. La Tupina has comfortable accommodation – you might fancy the erotic Orange Room.

MUST SEE/DO: Worth seeking out are the **Place de la Bourse** and **Pont de Pierre** (Napoleon's bridge), and for a great city walk, try the districts of **Sainte-Croix**, **Saint-Michel** and **Chartrons**. If you can handle a 2CV, hire from **La Voiture de Mon Père**. A good place for a swim is **Cap Ferrat** – if the tide's not too far out.

BERLIN

EATING OUT: Beginning with classic German cuisine, there's **Zur Letzten Instanz** for an overwhelmingly large *Eisbein* (page 252). A similarly gigantic version can be enjoyed at the **Hofbräuhaus**, grilled and served with lots of *Senf* (German mustard) and glorious Bavarian beer. There's a good food stand, **Konnopke's Imbiß**, which sells arguably Berlin's most famous fast food, *Currywurst*. Try cutting-edge cuisine at **Cookies Cream** – a high-end vegetarian restaurant in an alley behind the Westin Grand Hotel; very nice Parmesan dumplings there. My favourite restaurant name in Berlin is **Nobelhart & Schmutzig** (literally, 'Noble, Hard and Dirty'), where Billy Wagner presents dishes made with only local ingredients. Almost as enjoyable for the art as the food is **La Soupe Populaire**, where the paintings are changed regularly. Lovely dining room and great Michelin-starred cooking at Sonja Frühsammer's restaurant, just called **Frühsammers**. Reflecting the Turkish population are the great doner kebabs at **Hasir**.

SHOPPING: An excellent deli with a great selection of German wines, good cookery books (including my own!) and a demonstration kitchen is **Goldhahn & Sampson**.

WHERE TO STAY: Let's start with the mind-bendingly trendy **Hotel Bikini** in Budapester Straße, with a Mini Countryman, circa 1963, installed as a piece of art in the foyer. Sadly, we could only afford one night there. After that there's the **Novotel** – comfortable and centrally located. We managed a lunchtime cocktail at the elegant **Hotel Adlon** right by the Brandenburg Gate; would love to stay there.

MUST SEE/DO: The **Panoramapunkt** in Potsdamer Platz offers a brilliant view of the city, or so I'm told – the view was obscured by swirling snow when I was there. For a chilling experience, visit the **Berlin Wall** next to the excavated SS headquarters and the museum there. If you can work out the gear change, drive in a convoy of **Trabants** and listen to a guided commentary from a tinny speaker inside your spartan little car.

You must go to the giant department store, **KaDeWe**, and if you also visited **Bösebrücke** bridge and gazed on the site of the 1970s nightclub Dschungel, now the Ellington Hotel, you would be humming David Bowie's 'Where Are We Now?' for the rest of the weekend and feeling very *noir*.

REYKJAVIK

EATING OUT: There's an excellent Halibut Soup (page 158) to be had at **Matur og Drykkur**, among other great modern Icelandic dishes. Very cutting-edge, but good too, is **Dill Restaurant** – I liked the wild goose with crowberries; the langoustine bisque (page 57) at **Fjöruborðið** in Stokkseyri had a lovely deep shellfish flavour. You get a nice Cod Gratin (page 35) at **Grandakaffi** and decent hotdogs after a night in the pub at **Bæjarins Beztu Pylsur** – 'the best hotdog in town' (to translate the name), if maybe not the best in the world. If you want to try the famous disgusting food, it's **Sægreifinn** (Sea Baron) for stinky skate and the **Íslenski Barinn** (Icelandic Bar) for fermented shark and a shot of Brennivín. Good cod in a pan at the **Icelanddair Hotel Reykjavik Marina**, right on the harbour, and wild cocktails. **SHOPPING:** I bought my Icelandic sweater at **Nordic Store**.

MUST SEE/DO: You should go to **Hallgrímskirkja** Lutheran church, visible from wherever you are in the city. Its arresting steeple seems to sum up Nordic architecture and Icelandic sagas all in one building. You're bound to visit the world-famous **Strokkur** geyser – check the deep shade of turquoise just before it erupts. The **Gullfoss** waterfall on a day of snow and frost was arrestingly powerful. Sampling Icelandic rye bread baked in volcanic sand (page 129) at **Laugarvatn Fontana** spa was memorable, especially when eaten to the background aroma of sulphur. Take a dip in the secret lagoon with its 40°C water while you wait for your eggs to boil in a hot spring nearby. If you go in the winter, you'll be on alert from the hotel for the **Northern Lights** – which we missed, damn it!

VIENNA

EATING OUT: My favourite restaurant in Vienna is a little one, **Rudi's Beisl**, largely because owner and chef Christian Wanek is so full of life. Do try his pan-fried steak with crispy onion rings. For the perfect Wiener Schnitzel (page 198), it's got to be the **Hotel Imperial**. To experience the Austrian equivalent of roast beef and Yorkshire pudding, go for the Tafelspitz (page 254) at **Plachutta**. For the best Viennese Gulasch (page 195), **Meixner** is the place, and for really honest new Viennese cuisine, try **Petz**, particularly Christian Petz's *Grammelknödel*. You must try Stephanie Herkner's Sarma (page 274) at **Zur Herknerin**, too. You'll certainly want to visit a classic Viennese café; the two I liked were **Café Sperl** and **Café Landtmann**. You'll also want to have coffee and Sachertorte (page 114) – either at **Demel**, which also makes great Apfelstrudel (page 224), or at the **Hotel Sacher**. For delicious open sandwiches, go to **Trześniewski**; it's been there for a hundred years and is still incredibly busy.

SHOPPING: The **Naschmarkt**, Vienna's enormous and most famous market, is a must. Go to the sauerkraut seller there, **Leo Strmiska**, and a good vinegar shop, **Stand 111– 114**. There's a great sausage company called **Bitzinger** that has a number of stands around the city, notably the one by the opera house.

MUST SEE/DO: Vienna is stuffed full of fabulous buildings: the **Belvedere**, the **Secession Building**, even the **Academy of Fine Arts**, where Hitler failed to become a student. If you like your Graham Greene, the giant Ferris wheel, as featured in the film *The Third Man*, is at **Prater Park**, and for a completely and wonderfully over-the-top industrial plant, visit Hundertwasser's spectacular golden-chimneyed incinerator at **Spittelau**.

BOLOGNA

EATING OUT: For the best tortellini and tortelloni in town, it's **Le Sfogline**; for roast rabbit stuffed with frittata, **Ristorante Biassanot**; for gurnard with passatelli (page 295), **Ristorante Ciacco**; for soft onion Ravioli with Porcini Mushrooms, Sun-dried Tomatoes and Hazelnuts (page 89), **Scacco Matto**. Another place for great tortellini is **All'Osteria Bottega**. For a beautiful *crema di limone* ice cream, try **Cremeria Santo Stefano**, and for a smart place for coffee, the **Aroma** café.

SHOPPING: **Gino Fabbri**, a bakery and pastry shop on the outskirts of town, produces the best *colomba di Pasqua*, Easter cakes made with candied orange peel and baked in the shape of a dove. I loved Bologna's **Mercato della Erbe**, which in addition to wonderfully fresh produce, has some great restaurants. Go for grilled calamari stuffed with olive oil mash at **Banco 32**. For the best Balsamic vinegar, which is hardly vinegary at all, an hour away at Vignola, is **Acetaia dei Bago**.

WHERE TO STAY: The hotel where we stayed, **Corona d'Oro**, is lovely; just don't get claustrophobic on your way – you'll go through some of the narrowest streets ever navigated by a minibus. A short drive takes you to an incredibly rugged and attractive *agritourismo*, **La Fenice**, in the hills above the city.

MUST SEE/DO: Buildings you will love: the **Asinelli Tower** – go on, you have to climb it, even if you suffer a little from vertigo, as I do; the unfinished **San Petronio Basilica**, the main church, in the Piazza Maggiore; the **San Luca** basilica, with the world's longest portico (nearly two miles in length and with 666 arches); and back in Piazza Maggiore, the whispering gallery beneath the **Palazzo del Podestà**.

COPENHAGEN

EATING OUT: For new Nordic cuisine, I liked **Geranium**, Denmark's only restaurant with three Michelin stars – very elaborate but with great local flavours. **Kadeau** has similarly complicated dishes, all inspired by the Island of Bornholm, plus a fascinating collection of pickles – lovely restaurant looking like the smartest Scandinavian kitchen-cum-living area. **Den Røde Cottage** offers serious foraged food in a Hansel and Gretel-like cottage in the wood at Klampenborg. Nearby is Bellevue Beach with its blue-striped lifeguard towers and beach kiosks designed by Arne Jacobsen, creator of those famous wrap-around chairs. For good French/Danish food, try **Gammel Mønt**, once a brothel, which serves great turbot. Opposite is **Restaurationen**, offering similarly classic cooking, with an emphasis on local ingredients, and a fine wine list. For seafood *smørrebrød* (page 93), go to **Schønnemann**, and visit **Grøften**, the giant family restaurant in Tivoli Gardens, for fish cakes with tarragon remoulade sauce (page 29). For vegetarians, there's **Morgedstedet** in the hippy, self-governing free town of Christiania – the whole area feels like you've been transported back to 1969. **Mirabelle** is great for Danish pastries, sourdough bread (page 120) and coffee, while **Ved Stranden 10**, where I spoke to Sofie Gråbøl, is a pleasant and informal wine bar.

WHERE TO STAY: You might like a night or two at the floating **Hotel CPH Living**, made from a converted barge. Breakfast may come out of a machine, but the rooms are thoughtful modern Danish.

MUST SEE/DO: Hire a bicycle and ride to **Nyboder** to see the yellow houses. Mess about in the **harbour** in a GoBoat. Visit **Tolvahallerne** market, filled with great-quality stores, including a Mexican taco stand run by a former Noma chef. Go to **NY Carlsberg Glyptotek** (sculpture museum) – the personal collection of Carl Jacobsen, the son of the founder of the Carlsberg Brewery. If you love the Sydney Opera House, you'll enjoy visiting the church at **Bagsværd**, designed by Jørn Utzon.

CADIZ

EATING OUT: Seafood in Cadiz is excellent. For good fish restaurants, try: **El Faro** for *corvina a la plancha* (corvina is like the big brother of sea bass); **La Marea** for seafood and rice dishes like Arroz Verde (page 24); **Ventorillo el Chato** for Seared Almadraba Tuna with Red Wine (page 200); **Taberna el Tío de La Tiza** for al fresco dining and mackerel piriñaca (page 79); **Gadisushi** in the central market for Sashimi (page 162) of Almadraba tuna; **Casa Bigote** at Sanlúcar de Barrameda for *langostinos*, large local prawns; **Taberna del Chef del Mar** at El Puerto de Santa María for cuttlefish eggs with plankton in a green sauce that tastes like the sea; **El Arriate**, also at El Puerto, with a lovely courtyard and cuttlefish cooked on a plank. For bars and cafés: **Ultramar & Nos** for chickpea and chorizo stew (page 42) and Andalusian *jamon ibérico*; **El Faro** tapas bar for *fritura de pescado a la gaditana* and *tortillitas de camarones* (prawn fritters); **Casa Manteca** for chicharrones served thinly sliced on waxed paper; **Barbiana** in Sanlúcar de Barrameda for fabulous *papas aliñás* (Warm Potato Salad with

Tuna – page 296); **Bajamar**, next to the market in Cadiz, for *café con leche*, churros and hot chocolate for dipping them in (page 223); **Café Royalty** for afternoon tea – and Huevos a la Flamenca (page 82); the salt-of-the-earth **Taberna La Manzanilla** for a glass of sherry. **WHERE TO STAY: Playa Victoria** for a nice hotel, right on the beach, near La Marea fish restaurant. **MUST SEE/DO:** Visit the fish market at the **Mercado Central de Abastos** even if you're not buying anything – such a vivid array of fresh fish and shellfish. At **Bodegas Tradicíon** in Jerez de la Frontera, you can sample some truly wonderful sherries and enjoy a gallery full of priceless art. For flamenco, go to **Peña Flamenca la Perla**.

LISBON

EATING OUT: João do Grão for Pork and Clams Alentejo-style (page 80). **Solar dos Nunes** for earthy country cooking, again from Alentejo, in the Algave. **Casa do Peixe**, on the first floor of the Saldanha market, for grilled sardines, and **Valenciana** for Chicken Piri-Piri (page 74) – perfect if you're feeling ravenous. **Moma Grill**, a very untouristy restaurant right in the heart of the city, for Iberian pork strip cooked on charcoal and a lovely Douro red wine – Quinta dos Acipestes. **Cervejaria Ramiro** for seafood and beer plus a *prego* (veal sandwich). **Casa da India** for grilled chicken, squid and atmosphere. **Pérola de São Paulo** for Octopus Salad (page 163). **Tasca do Chico** for fado and good Caldo Verde (page 277). **Ponto Final**, at Almada, overlooking the River Tagus and Lisbon, for tomato rice and tapas-like appetizers. **Porto de Santa Maria**, on the Guincho beach, for fish baked in bread, seafood rice and Almond Tart (page 220). **Restaurante da Adraga**, Sintra, for seafood on a lovely beach reminiscent of north Cornwall, and a great fizzy Vinho Verde. **SHOPPING: Mercado da Ribeira** market has been transformed under the Time Out brand into a food hall with restaurants, wine and cook shops. Buy Pastéis de Nata (page 107), hot from the oven at **Pastéis de Belém**. For tinned sardines, go to **Conserveira de Lisboa**, and, for Salt Cod Fritters (page 144), **Versailles** at Terminal 1 in the airport. **Feira da Ladra** is Lisbon's flea market.

WHERE TO STAY: We stayed at **Avenida Palace**; going up the stairs, my wife Sas commented on how one floor looked very like the portal in *Being John Malkovitch*. **MUST SEE/DO: Belém Tower** and the **Discovery Monument**; Sintra and **Adraga Beach; Jerónimos Monastery; Calouste Gulbenkian** and **Berardo** museums. Watch out for beautiful old tiles everywhere – particularly in the **Palace of Sintra**.

THESSALONIKI

EATING OUT: Sempriko, an enterprising informal place near the law courts, for buffalo kebabs. **Xontro Alati** for Soutzoukakia (page 64) and grilled tomato salad with Kalamata balsamic vinegar (page 175). **To Elliniko** for Mussel Pilaf (page 28), Fava Santorini (page 150) and divine onions stuffed with minced lamb and pine nuts. **Tsarouchas** for tripe soup with chilli oil, Artichoke Stew (page 71) and chicken with avgolemono sauce. **Marina** taverna for great squid *souvlaki* (page 265). **Ta Bakaliarakia Tou Aristou**, a fish and chip place, but offering top-quality salt cod with fried potatoes (page 67), skordalia and fried chillies. **Doukas** taverna, at Chalastra, miles off the beaten track, for pilaf with mussels straight out of the water and slow-cooked cuttlefish. At Epanomi, a beach taverna called **Agyrovoli** for grilled sun-dried octopus and whole sea bass split open and grilled. The **Olympion** for great Negronis and music; we were there most nights after work. **SHOPPING: Bantis Bougatsa** for Kima Bougatsa (page 61). **Terkenlis** bakery for *tsoureki* (brioche) flavoured with mastic and cherry kernels, crenulated little cakes called *touloumpakia*, and mini *galactoboureko*. **Pantopoli** ('The Grocer') is a delight for any food lover – the best Greek produce and a labyrinth of goods from further afield, including Kozani saffron. **Mia Feta** for organic feta: true feta should be 70 per cent sheep's milk and 30 per cent goat's. **Kepani** market for fish, cheese and loukaniko sausages. **WHERE TO STAY:** The stylish **Electra Palace**, built in the 1950s; I loved the marble staircases and curved corridors and the view over Aristotelous Square to the Thermaikos Gulf. The **Excelsior** nearby is smart and comfortable. **MUST SEE/DO: Galerius Arch, Rotunda, White Towe, Ano Poli**

(the old town), *Umbrellas* (sculpture by Giorgos Zogolopoulos). Head to the **Halkidiki** beaches for swimming. **Ouzerie Tbourlika** and **Prigkipesa** for rebetiko music and dancing.

PALERMO

EATING OUT: Gagini Social Restaurant has helpful staff and a little tricksy but sound cooking. I had red mullet with crushed broccoli, pine nuts, sun-dried tomatoes and black cuttlefish juice. **Bisso Bistrot** in the old Libreria Dante by the Quattro Canti for broccoli with pasta and very reasonable prices, and **Trattoria ai Cascinari** for pasta with fresh tuna and wild fennel. I went to **Trattoria Basile** because they served Panelle (page 151) and spleen sandwiches – all good, honest home cooking. Loved the caponata. **Carlo V**, a small restaurant in a piazza just off the Ballarò market, for ceviche of tuna. **Ferro di Cavallo** for *polpette di sarde*, and **Trattoria di Corona** for anchovy and orange fish balls. **Spinnato** for light lunches, coffee granita, cannoli and people watching. **Cappello** for Martorana (marzipan fruit) and cassata, and **Gelateria Brioscia** for ice cream in freshly baked brioche (page 236). Restaurant and B&B **Simpaty**, at Mondello, for sea urchin risotto and fish in *acqua pazza* (crazy water). For a drink, there's **Taverna Azzurra**, always packed, in the Vucciria market, and **A'Cala** in the old harbour. For good street food, look for Sfincione (page 155); chickpea fritters in buns; *stigghiola* (lamb or calf intestines grilled and served with lemon); *frittula* (crisp veal bits); *pani câ mèusa* (spleen sandwiches). **KePalle** for takeaway dishes. **SHOPPING: Mercato del Capo** has Dickensian alleyways and plenty of street food, while **Ballarò** market is great for fish, vegetables and offal, its meandering streets lined with plywood stalls. Visit **La Vucciria**: narrow streets of relentless energy, the bars overflowing and lots of good restaurants and places to stay. **Enoteca Picone** for wine. **WHERE TO STAY:** The **Grand Hotel Villa Igiea** has amazing art nouveau interiors. **MUST SEE/DO: Monreale**; *The Triumph of Death* at **Palazzo Abatellis**; Palermo Cathedral; the church of **Santa Maria dell'Ammiraglio**, Martorana; **Cappella Palatina** (the royal chapel of the Norman kings of Sicily) for the mosaics. Read *The Leopard* by Giuseppe Tomasi di Lampedusa.

EXTRAS

CHICKEN STOCK
Makes about 1.5 litres

Bones from 1.5kg chicken or 500g
   chicken wings, uncooked, or
   leftovers from a roast chicken
1 large carrot, roughly chopped
2 sticks celery, roughly sliced
2 leeks, washed and sliced
2 fresh or dried bay leaves
2 sprigs thyme
2.5 litres water

Put all the ingredients in a large
pan and bring up to the boil,
skimming off any scum that rises
to the surface. Leave to simmer
gently for about 2 hours – it is
important not to let it boil as this
will form an emulsion between
the fat and the water and make
the stock cloudy. Strain through
a fine or muslin-lined sieve and
use as required. If not using
immediately, leave to cool,
then refrigerate or freeze.

For a brown chicken stock,
roast the bones and vegetables
in the oven for 30 to 45 minutes
at 220°C/gas 7 before simmering.

BEEF STOCK &
CONCENTRATED
BEEF STOCK
Makes about 2.4 litres

2 tbsp vegetable oil
2 celery sticks, roughly chopped
2 carrots, roughly chopped
2 onions, roughly chopped
900g shin of beef
5 litres water
2 bay leaves
2 sprigs thyme
1 tbsp salt

For a pale brown stock, put all
the ingredients except the bay
leaves, thyme and salt into a
large pan and bring to the boil,
skimming off the scum that rises

to the surface. Simmer for 4
hours, adding the salt and herbs
for the last 15 minutes. Strain
through a fine or muslin-lined
sieve into a clean pan. If not
using immediately, leave to
cool, then refrigerate or freeze.

For a richer-tasting, concentrated
stock, heat the oil in the pan, add
the vegetables and beef and fry
for 10 to 15 minutes until nicely
browned. Add the water and
continue as above, adding
the herbs and salt 15 minutes
before the end of cooking.

FISH STOCK
Makes about 1.2 litres

1kg fish bones, such as lemon
   sole, brill and plaice
1 onion, chopped
1 fennel bulb, chopped
100g celery, sliced
100g carrot, chopped
25g button mushrooms, sliced
1 sprig thyme
2.5 litres water

Put all the ingredients in a
large pan and simmer gently
for 30 minutes. Strain through
a fine or muslin-lined sieve.
If not using immediately, leave
to cool, then refrigerate or freeze.

VEGETABLE STOCK
Makes about 2 litres

2 large onions
2 large carrots
1 head celery
1 bulb fennel
1 bulb garlic
Handful thyme sprigs
3 bay leaves
1 tsp salt
15g dried porcini
   mushrooms
3 litres water

Peel and slice the vegetables; you
don't need to peel the garlic. Put
everything in a large pan with the
water and bring to the boil. Simmer
for an hour, then strain through
a fine or muslin-lined sieve. If not
using immediately, leave to cool,
then refrigerate or freeze.

DUCK OR GOOSE FAT CHIPS
Serves 4

600g floury potatoes,
   such as Maris Piper
   or King Edwards, peeled
2 x 320g jars duck or goose fat
Salt

Cut the potatoes into 5mm-thick
slices, then lengthways into chips.
Rinse under cold running water
and dry on a tray lined with a
clean tea towel.

Heat the duck or goose fat in a
large pan to 120°C; the pan should
be no more than a third full. Cook
the chips in batches for 4 to 5
minutes until tender but not
coloured. Remove from the fat
and set aside until ready to serve.

To finish the chips, heat the oil
to 190°C and cook in batches for
about 2 minutes until golden and
crisp. Drain on kitchen paper
and sprinkle with salt.

SAUTÉ POTATOES
Serves 4

750g floury potatoes, peeled
   and cut into 4cm pieces
40g butter
3 tbsp olive oil
Sprig rosemary, leaves chopped
   (optional)
Salt and pepper

Put the potatoes into a pan of
salted water (1 tsp per 600ml),
bring to the boil and simmer until

tender, about 7 minutes. Drain well and leave until the steam has dispersed.

Heat the butter and oil in a large, heavy-based frying pan. It's important not to overcrowd the pan, so use 2 pans if necessary. Add the potatoes and fry over medium heat until crisp, golden brown and sandy – the outside of the potatoes should break off a little as you sauté them to give a nice crumbly crust. Add the rosemary, if using, after a few minutes. Season with salt and pepper and serve.

PILAF RICE
Serves 4

60g finely chopped onion
30g butter
350g long-grain rice
600ml water or stock
1 tsp salt

Cook the onion gently in the butter for 1–2 minutes, then stir in the rice. Add the liquid and salt. Bring to the boil, then cover and simmer for about 15 minutes. For variety, add your choice of about 60g nuts, seeds or currants with the rice.

POLITIKI
Serves 4 to 6

175g white cabbage, finely shredded
175g red cabbage, finely shredded
2 large carrots, grated
4 red peppers, roasted,
    skinned, sliced
Small handful flat-leaf
    parsley, chopped
2 tbsp baby capers

For the dressing
80ml extra-virgin Greek olive oil
30ml red wine vinegar
1 tbsp coarse grain Dijon mustard
1 clove garlic, grated or
    finely chopped
½ tsp salt

Make the dressing by whisking together the oil, vinegar, mustard, garlic and salt.

Mix all the prepared vegetables in a large bowl, dress them and serve.

MOJO PICÓN
Makes 1 small jar

6 cloves garlic, chopped
2 red jalapeño chillies,
    seeded and chopped
1 tsp cumin seeds
½ tsp salt
1 tsp sweet smoked paprika
    (*pimentón dulce*)
3 tbsp sherry vinegar
12 tbsp olive oil
4 tbsp breadcrumbs,
    soaked in 2 tbsp water

In a food processor or blender, blitz the garlic with the chilli, cumin seeds and salt until you have a paste. Add the paprika, vinegar, olive oil and breadcrumbs, and a little more water to let down the consistency if it's too thick. Store in a clean jam jar. Keeps for about a week in the fridge.

MUSTARD MAYONNAISE
Makes 150ml

1 egg yolk
1 tsp mustard
1 tsp lemon juice
Pinch salt
125ml vegetable oil (rapeseed oil)

Make the mayonnaise in a bowl by mixing the egg yolk with mustard, lemon juice and salt, then gradually add the vegetable oil, stirring continuously, until all the oil is incorporated.

ALIOLI
Makes about 175ml

4 cloves garlic, peeled
½ tsp fine table salt
1 medium egg yolk
175ml extra-virgin olive oil

Crush the garlic cloves on a board under the blade of a large knife. Add the salt and work with the side of the blade to form a smooth, salty paste. Scrape into a liquidizer or food processor and add the egg yolk. Turn on the machine and very slowly trickle the oil through the hole in the lid until you have a thick emulsion. Keeps in the fridge for at least a week.

TOMATO SAUCE
Makes about 600ml

6 tbsp olive oil
4 cloves garlic, finely
    chopped or grated
1kg well-flavoured tomatoes
    or 2 x 400g tins plum tomatoes
Salt and pepper

Heat the olive oil in a saucepan over medium heat, then add the garlic and gently cook for a couple of minutes. Add the tomatoes, salt and pepper, reduce the heat and cook very gently for 40 minutes, breaking up the tomatoes with a wooden spoon as they cook, until the sauce has thickened. Add a little water if it becomes dry. If you want a smooth sauce, blend it in a liquidizer.

If not using immediately, leave to cool, then refrigerate or freeze. I always keep a bag of tomato sauce in the freezer.

SAUERKRAUT
Allow 5 to 7 days, start to finish, to make this true fermented sauerkraut.

1kg (prepared weight) white
    or red cabbage, outer leaves
    removed, central tough
    core removed
1 tbsp fine sea salt
1 tsp caraway seeds

Grate or finely chop the cabbage and put in a roomy bowl. (Grating means the cabbage will yield liquid more quickly.) Sprinkle over the salt and caraway seeds, and massage until liquid flows freely from the cabbage. This could take up to 10 minutes. Pack the mixture in a clean 1-litre Kilner jar and compress so that the cabbage is submerged. Ensure there is a gap of about 5cm at the top of the jar. Close the lid and leave in a cool but not cold place out of direct sunlight to ferment for 5 days. Open the jar every couple of days to allow the mixture to 'burp', i.e. allow gases to be released.

It is now ready to eat, although it may continue to improve over the next day or two. At this point store it in the fridge to slow down the fermentation process. It will keep for up to six months stored in a fridge.

You can vary the spices, substituting fennel seeds, cumin seeds or juniper berries, although caraway is the most traditional. As a rule of thumb, for every 1kg cabbage use 1 tablespoon salt and 1 teaspoon spice.

PICKLED CABBAGE LEAVES

You need a Kilner jar of 1.5 litres. For the brine, add 2 tablespoons of salt to 1.2 litres of water and stir to dissolve; add 1 teaspoon caraway seeds. Carefully peel at least 8 of the large outer leaves off a white cabbage and cut a 'v' out of the tough central stem. Roll the large leaves and place them in the jar. Slot in the scraps, then pour in the brine to the top. Seal the jar and store at room temperature for 5 to 7 days, opening briefly every day or so to prevent a build-up of gases. After this time, they are ready for use. At this point they can also be stored in the sealed jar in the fridge (without being 'burped'), where they will keep for a month. Drain well before use.

SOURDOUGH STARTER

Flours vary, kitchen temperatures fluctuate, ovens differ and starters are living things, so it is hard to be too precise about quantities. It's a case of trial and error the first couple of times you bake, but you will soon know what works for you. You need a 1-litre Kilner-style jar, water and rye flour.

Day 1
Mix 30g wholegrain rye flour with 60ml warm water, stir well and leave with lid ajar for 24 hours in a warm kitchen.

Day 2
Add a further 30g flour and 60ml water, stir well and leave with lid ajar for another 24 hours in a warm kitchen.

Day 3
Add another 30g flour and 60ml water and leave as before.

Day 4
By this stage the starter should be doubling or tripling in bulk each day. Feed again as before with 30g flour and 60ml water.

Day 5
Today your starter should be bubbly and active and ready to use.

Starter maintenance
Rye starter is not quite as needy as wheat flour starter and can be fed less often. Feed every 3 or 4 days if baking regularly, with the quantities as above.

If you are not baking regularly, you can store the starter in the fridge. Discard half the mixture every week or two and add 40g rye flour and 70ml warm water. Allow it bubble and activate before refrigerating again. Always allow it to come up to room temperature and start bubbling again before using.

DILL OIL
Makes about 150ml

150ml rapeseed or sunflower oil
1 large bunch fresh dill

In a food processor, blend the oil and dill together until the dill is very finely chopped and the oil is bright green. Strain into a clean jam jar. Keeps in the fridge for at least a week.

BREADCRUMBS
Heat the oven to 140°C/gas 1. Process crustless white bread in a food processor into crumbs. Spread over a large baking tray and bake for 20 minutes, then stir the crumbs and bake for a further 15 to 20 minutes until uniformly crisp and dried but not browned. Leave to cool, then store in an airtight container. They keep very well.

CLARIFIED BUTTER
Melt butter in a small pan over low heat. The object is to boil off the liquids which form the emulsion that is butter. Allow it to bubble, which is the water escaping as steam. As this subsides take off the heat and leave the remaining solids to settle, then pour the clear golden butter oil through a fine sieve into a bowl. Keeps in the fridge for at least a week.

BEURRE MANIÉ
Blend equal quantities of butter and plain flour together into a smooth paste. Cover and keep in the fridge until needed. It will keep as long as butter. Whisk into hot sauces to thicken them.

COOK'S TIPS

All teaspoon and tablespoon measurements are level unless otherwise specified, and are based on measuring spoons:

1 teaspoon = 5ml
1 tablespoon = 15ml

Readers in Australia need to make a minor adjustment as their tablespoon measure is 20ml.

It's often useful to be precise with measurements until you get the idea of a dish, then you can always adapt it to suit yourself.

Cooking times are approximate. All oven temperatures are standard; reduce by 10–20°C if using a fan oven.

EGGS
All eggs are medium unless otherwise specified; use at room temperature. I recommend using cage-free, free-range eggs.

BUTTER
Butter is salted unless otherwise specified.

CHICKEN
All chicken recipes are skin-on unless otherwise specified. I recommend free-range chicken.

GARLIC AND ONIONS
With the arrival of microplanes I don't bother to skin or crush garlic these days. I grate a clove of garlic with the skin on; the garlic grates, the skin doesn't. The easiest way to peel a clove of garlic is to cut a sliver off the root end of the clove which usually takes the papery skin with it; if not, a gentle tap with the flat side of a knife should do it. An average clove of garlic weighs 3–5g.

As a general rule of thumb for unpeeled weights:

1 small shallot = 25g
1 small onion = 100g
1 medium onion = 175g
1 large onion = 225g

TEMPERATURE PROBE
I always use a temperature probe to determine the correct internal temperature of meat, poultry, game or fish. This is a cheap gadget and you will get far more accurate results with one than by relying on cooking times alone. The temperatures below are just before taking off the heat.

Meat, duck, goose and game:
Rare 50°C
Medium rare 55°C
Medium 60°C
Medium well done 65°C
Well done 70°C

Chicken is ready at 65°C.

Fish ranges from very rare in the centre at 45°C for oily fish such as salmon and tuna, through to moist at 55°C, to no blood on the bones for a whole fish at 60°C.

Meat and fish continue to cook after being removed from the heat; their temperature rises by about 6°C. Meat and poultry benefit from resting for 15 minutes after being cooked and before being served.

HARD-TO-SOURCE INGREDIENTS
Pimentón, salt cod, chorizo, paella rice and pans, churros extruders: try thetapaslunchcompany.co.uk

Wakame dried seaweed: try health food shops, Asian supermarkets or online suppliers

Anelletti pasta: try valvonacrolla.co.uk and gastronicks.co.uk

Liquorice powder: try health food shops, Scandinavian Tiger stores and online

INDEX

ACKNOWLEDGEMENTS

I love writing cookery books. It's not a solitary activity, like writing a memoir; it's about working with a team, which is lots of fun Actually, there are two teams: the book one, Ebury; and the TV one, Denham Productions. I would like to thank the two people who work in both: Portia Spooner, who has put so much hard work into collating and testing all the recipes in this book, in close collaboration with everyone at Denhams, including preparing all the food for the cooking filmed at my cottage in Padstow; and Arezoo Farahazad, who has worked tirelessly to give Portia so much back-up, including writing down recipes of all the dishes being cooked while filming on location, and sending them straight back to Portia for testing.

At Ebury, I would like to thank Rebecca Smart, the MD, Lizzy Gray, Publishing Director, and Charlotte Macdonald, Editor, with whom I've worked on an almost daily basis recently and have enjoyed it very much. I'd also like to thank Claire Scott, my long suffering publicist at Ebury, who I note I've been working with great enjoyment for 16 years. The lynchpin between me and the publisher, though, has been my long-standing (eleven years) copy-editor, Mari Roberts. Thanks for the pinpoint attention to detail, making the recipes so clear and accurate.

For their vital role in making *Long Weekends* look so lovely, thanks to Alex and Emma Smith, who designed it, and James Murphy, who took every one of the beautiful photographs and with whom I've now been working for seventeen years. Also thanks to Aya Nishimura for her beautiful food preparation and Penny Markham for so expertly matching the pots, plates and pans for the food photography from so many weekend cities.

For *Long Weekends*, the TV programme, thanks to David Pritchard and for all we've done together over the last twenty-five years. It goes on being a delight to work with someone so creative and talented. Thanks, too, to my TV family: Chris Topliss, a great cameraman, and Pete Underwood, our sound recordist, who's a bit like a bass guitarist – very good, and essential, but not often recognized as such. Then there's Martin Willcocks, on second camera; Adam de Wan, Suki Hughs and Richard Atkinson, our editors; Tom Edwards, dubbing mixer; Grace Kitto, who runs Denhams, and Chris Denham, aka the Major, whose company it is.

Not forgetting a few occasional helpers: Henry Morris and my stepson Zach Burns, both tripod carrying in the hot Greek sun; Paul Ashton, who rigged the cottage; and Rob Jones, who put in time testing recipes in Padstow. Also the programme researchers at Denhams: Fiona Pritchard, Dave's wife, and Jemma Woodman, Elizabeth Stone, Charlotte Barton and Claudia Selby.

Finally, a big thank-you to Viv Taylor and Jane Reese for coordinating everything in Padstow.

All these credits would be still running as the cinema was emptying, but I always wait till it says where the film was made, so I would see this: I would like to thank my dear wife, Sas, who came with me to every city and added so much colour to the whole book. You need to go with someone who you love on a long weekend.